Revolutions for Fun and Profit!

The Proletariat's Guide to Political Uprisings, Citizen Revolutions and Personal Hygiene

by Ryan Shattuck

Bullshattuck Publishing
Salt Lake City, Utah

FIRST EDITION: August 2009

Designed by Lani Dame

Library of Congress Cataloging-in-Publication Data has been applied for.

ISBN 978-0-578-03482-9
LCCN: 2009907961

Published in the United States of America

Dedicated to Dick & Denny.
And other revolutionaries.

A WARNING ABOUT THIS BOOK

The book you are about to enjoy is very offensive. In fact, it should probably be banned by most libraries and churches. For that reason, I've printed this book on extremely flammable paper, should you decide to take that route. You're welcome.

The reason this book is so offensive is because it is all about revolutions. As you may be surprised to learn, revolutions are not a very pleasant topic to discuss in front of polite company. Many revolutions are filled with murder. OFFENSIVE. Occasionally revolutions deal with kidnappings. OFFENSIVE. And some revolutions are even made in Taiwan. OFFENSIVE.

As you can see, these are very unsavory topics. But it doesn't just stop there. There is language in this book that may offend your sensitivities, such as the word "bitch," the word "bullshit," and the most offensive language of all, "German."

Revolutions often tend to be critical of some forms of government, of corporations, or some religions. Don't be offended then, when you discover that this book mocks people from all religions, including Christians, Jews, and Muslims. It doesn't however mock Scientologists, because the belief that the human race descended from space aliens is no laughing matter.

If after reading this warning you decide that this book is too offensive, I will understand. Perhaps you might enjoy *Cats in Quilts: 14 Purrfect Projects* (ISBN-13: 978-1571201751) instead.

What if you decide that you DO want to read the most revolutionary book of your lifetime?

Consider yourself warned.

TABLE OF CONTENTS
★ ★ ★ ★ ★

★ ★ ★

SECTION I
A HISTORY OF REVOLUTIONS: COWARDICE, CON MEN, AND COMPLACENCY

★ ★ ★

SECTION II
EMBRACE THE HATE: LEARNING TO LOVE THE INNER REVOLUTIONARY

★ ★ ★
SECTION III
THE BRASS TACKS OF A REVOLUTION: BECAUSE SOMEBODY BROKE THE STAPLER

★ ★ ★

"A revolution is a fundamental change in power or organization structure that takes place in a relatively short period of time. ... Revolutions have occurred throughout human history and vary widely in terms of methods, duration, and motivating ideology. Their results include major changes in culture, economy, and socio-political institutions."

— from the Wikipedia entry for "Revolutions"

Feel free to edit this page if you believe this is incorrect.

FOREWORD BY KRISTEN HINTZ & JEREMIAH KNIGHT

★ ★ ★

Ryan Meredith Shattuck is often referred to as the Hitler of comedy. He is also known as the Mussolini of cheese danishes, but that's unimportant.

For the past forty years, Ryan has been perfecting the art of comedy. As a wildly unpopular stand-up comic, an editor of a wildly unpopular satirical Web site, and a wildly unpopular member of the Shattuck family, Ryan gained all the skills necessary to become a wildly unpopular self-published author.

For years, young Ryan took banjo lessons in the hope of becoming more like his idol (and the first person to issue a restraining order against him), Steve Martin. Much to his dismay, he discovered that no matter how hard he practiced, nobody wanted to hear him play the banjo. Not even his banjo teacher, which was not only ironic but a little sad. From this hardship, Ryan learned a valuable lesson. When it came to his unique brand of comedy, which he calls Comedygold™, Ryan had to focus first and foremost on his audience.

Since the decision to put his audience first, Ryan has found great success with his comedy. Of course, his audience usually consists of just himself and a bottle of wine. But regardless, Ryan and his bottle of wine think Ryan and his Comedygold™ are absolutely hilarious. For the first time, Ryan was popular. With himself. Provided he was drunk. So essentially, he was ridiculously popular. Ryan decided that this newfound popularity proved that the world was primed and ready for his first book.

The topic of this book came easily. Ryan's love for comedy was second only to his love of history, particularly in the historical components of revolutions. Himself a child of the American Revolution, Ryan had long been fascinated with revolutionary figures. He immersed himself in books about Guevara, King, Nietzsche, and, for some reason, Kurt Russell. He poured through books about all the most important revolutions in history to find the most humorous anecdotes he could use for his book.

What Ryan discovered was that there is really nothing all that funny about revolutions. Most result in turmoil, grief, and bloodshed. Undeterred, Ryan decided that if history would not accommodate him, he would invent his own history. He would stick to the essentials of Comedygold™, and simply make facts up to suit his own purposes.

And so we have *Revolutions for Fun and Profit!* A book all about facts Ryan Shattuck made up, assisted by his best friend, a bottle of wine.

—Kristen Hintz

Ryan's great.

—Jeremiah Knight

A FRIENDLY, YET REVOLUTIONARY LETTER FROM THE AUTHOR
★ ★ ★

Dearest Reader,

Good evening. Or morning, as the case may be.

I'd like to thank you for purchasing and/or borrowing and/or stealing this book from an associate and/or public library and/or book seller, for you hold in your hand(s) a complete and unabridged guide for the burgeoning revolutionary. You may now prepare yourself for the revolution of a lifetime. You are about to change the world.

This is true; the world is changing, and just one person will be responsible for this change — YOU. In our modern world of fast cars and loose change, one simply needs to look around to recognize that inequality and injustice prevail in even the smallest crevices of society. Who will ensure that women get the right to vote, that gay men get the right to marry, and that children get the right to do neither, due to those pesky labor laws?

YOU. The revolutionary.

As you will soon learn, revolutions are the catalyst for the progress in our world. Now, I recognize that you may not be familiar with the term, "revolutions." You may also be under the impression that revolutions consist entirely of drum circles, ice cream socials, and communal sex. This is factually incorrect. Statistically speaking, less than a quarter of all revolutions include some combination of drum circles, ice cream socials, and communal sex, public or private.

"I'm interested; sign me up for the revolution!" Wait just a minute. Like old-fashioned alchemy or whittling miniature Lincoln death masks out of hotel bar soap, hosting your own revolution is rather difficult. You may have to furrow your brow. You may have to program your VCR/TiVo hybrid to record your favorite television shows. Sacrifice will be required! Now I recognize that you, dear reader, may feel discouraged. You may feel depressed and consider ending your life because you believe that all of the good causes have already been revolted for and you have little to offer. Pull yourself together! As you will later learn, this is not so.

So sally forth, gentle reader! You say you want a revolution? Then turn off *Dancing With the Stars*, put down the cheese doodles, and put on your Birkenstocks — I'm going to make you into a revolutionary. Let the wind be at your back and your enemies at your feet. Short enemies.

In the immortal words of the late Susan B. Anthony, "Git-r-done!"

Hugs and kisses,[1]

Ryan Shattuck

1. Platonically, of course

WHAT YOU WILL FIND IN THIS BOOK

REVOLUTIONARY TRIVIA
Entertaining facts and trivia that are sure to make you the life of any party! Only works if everyone's been drinking.

IN THEIR OWN REVOLUTIONARY WORDS
Don't just take my word as gospel, although I'm flattered by those who do. Read what actual revolutionaries have said on the subject.

REVOLUTIONARY QUIZZES
This is simply to make sure that you've been paying attention.

REVOLUTIONARY GRAPHS AND CHARTS
If a single picture is worth a thousand words, then a bar graph must only be worth something like seventeen words, because when was the last time you saw a framed bar graph in the Louvre?[2]

2. Although I am told they do have a fine collection of late-Baroque pie charts.

REVOLUTIONARY CHECKLISTS
You finally have a reason to use the ballpoint pen that you've been keeping in the cupboard all those years.

REVOLUTIONARY COFFEE STAINS
Please be more careful.

REVOLUTIONARY TORN PAGES
We understand that you were babysitting your nephew, but books about revolutions are not meant to be children's playthings.

REVOLUTIONARY BOOKMARK FROM THE PREVIOUS LIBRARY PATRON
What is this, a cigarette?

YOUR MISSING CAR KEYS
Why are they always in the last place you look?

A History of Revolutions: Cowardice, Conmen and Complacency

1 a brief account of revolutions, revolutionaries and related astrological signs throughout history: abridged

3.Please don't sue me if you're The Beatles. Or if you're anybody else for that matter.

You say you want a revolution?[3] How nice for you. And what type of revolution do you want? An Upper Paleolithic revolution? An abortive socialist revolution? You have no idea, do you? You just happen to like the song by The Beatles, and that's good enough for you. Think you know everything there is to know about the history of revolutions? You don't. And not by a long shot.

Even if you posses a degree in revolutionology and had spent the better half of your life studying the history of revolutions, you still wouldn't know everything there is to know; like the glorious monarch butterfly, history is inconsistent and is constantly evolving. In fact, many people are surprised to learn that history also has a larval stage.[4]

Unbeknownst to much of the public, historians no longer attempt to record the stories and experiences of the revolutionaries that have fundamentally impacted world history. Simply put, revolutionaries do not want people to keep records about them. While records certainly exist of the comings and goings of revolutionaries, these are always produced from a third person point of view, as most have been made against the strict wishes of said revolutionaries.

Why is this — why this desire by revolutionaries to not be remembered? Many theories have been postulated. Some revolutionary historical theorists — or revoluhistorists — have theorized that this desire to remain anonymous is simply a noble request on behalf of the revolutionary to make a positive social change, without having to concern oneself with the repercussions of gratitude.

Another theory about why revolutionaries wishing to remain anonymous, states that this makes it easier for the revolutionary to get away with all sorts of crap.[5]

Let's say, for example, that you're technological revolutionary Bill Gates, and you change your order at a restaurant from chicken to fish. Not very easy to do, without the rumor mills going into overload, claiming that you've officially changed your diet from regular meat-eater to that of a pescetarian,[6] and thus all computers running Windows will inevitably crash. Now let's say you're Joe Nobody, and

4. It also eats milkweed.

5. Like square dancing

6. Seriously. It's a word.

you change your order at a restaurant from chicken to fish — after murdering a few people during a revolution. "I'm sorry Mr. Nobody, but we're out of fish. What's that you say? You just murdered a few people in the name of some fill-in-the-blank revolution? That's great, Mr. Nobody. More wine?"

You can't even blow your nose, when you're Bill Gates. You can murderously revolt against oppressive noses, when you're Joe Nobody and it won't even make the newspaper.

Some revolutionaries actually take preventative measures to keep their records secret. No one really knows what happened to Joan of Arc, for example, as she burned all

A REVOLUTIONARY FUN FACT!

The word "revolution" was named after Hubert de Revolution. Hubert — or "Bitch Tits," as he was known to his friends — was born in Spain in 1843. After working at a factory for over a decade, Hubert eventually grew tired of the dismal conditions — and furious over the cancellation of Casual Friday — and led his coworkers on a successful revolt against factory owners. Previous to this event, the term "revolution" did not exist and such revolutionaries had no way of demonstrating their desire to "stick it to the man."

Thanks to Hubert de Revolution, as well as his contemporary, Jose Political Uprising, we now enjoy the privilege of getting mad as hell and not taking it anymore.

In addition to wearing jeans every Friday.

factual records about her life with her at the stake.[7]

As such, the following history may or may not be "correct" or "accurate" in terms of historical revolutionaries who "may" or "may not have," at the very least, "existed." I have done my best to research the history of revolutions and their subsequent revolutionaries, but where blanks were found, blanks were filled. If I read a passage that said: "Mahatma Gandhi favored the _____ type of revolution," then I assumed "Mahatma Gandhi favored the incredibly violent type of revolution." Etc, etc, etc.

The rest, as they say, is history. Or as a revolutionary historical theorist might put it, "revoluhistoristy."

REVOLUTIONS THROUGHOUT HISTORY

In the beginning, God created the heavens and the earth. He then created Man and Woman. Only minutes after He created them, did Man and Woman revolt against God in an attempt to demonstrate that there's nothing the bourgeoisie cannot do when united in a common goal. God then struck down the revolutionaries with a fierce punishment, and that is why we no longer have tails.

From Day One, revolutions have played an important part in history. They've been responsible for good, they've been responsible for evil, and they've been responsible for bringing second-rate television shows back to life. The role of revolutionary truly is the world's oldest profession. Now some may argue that the "world's oldest profession" is

7. How's that for irony, John of Lancaster, 1st Duke of Bedford!

that of prostitute, but this is simply untrue. Not only is the revolutionary the world's oldest profession, but unlike a prostitute, most revolutionaries don't charge by the hour.[8]

It's true that unlike a corset, revolutions are not one-size-fits-all, nor are they as comfortable. Some people revolt against the government (a political revolution), while others revolt against corn (an agricultural revolution). Before an aspiring revolutionary starts his or her own revolution, he or she must first learn about the various types of revolutions that have occurred in the past. You wouldn't go on a blind date with somebody without Googling their name and performing an exhaustive background check on them, would you? The same goes for a revolutionary — you must learn about the revolution that you're joining before you actually start the revolution.

Although there are as many variations of revolutions as there are grains of sand on a beach, I have decided to include here only fifteen variations, thus making for very large grains of sand on a very small beach.[9] Revolutions fall

8. But they will steal your wallet.

9. There isn't even enough room to play midget beach volleyball.

A REVOLUTIONARY FUN FACT!

Did you know that the Scottish Agricultural Revolution was the inspiration behind a Lifetime Original Movie?

While I've never actually seen it, and aren't entirely sure what it's about, I do know that the guy in the movie probably gets what's coming to him.

---

into three primary categories: "Political/Socioeconomic Revolutions," "Intellectual/Philosophical/Technological Revolutions," and "Miscellaneous Revolutions." A fourth category may also be applied with crazy glue and good old-fashioned moxie.

POLITICAL/SOCIOECONOMIC REVOLUTIONS

Political Revolutions

Political revolutions are revolutions in which one form of government is replaced with another form of government, as was the case with the French Revolution. These types of revolutions will be the primary focus of this book. Political revolutions are often favored by anarchists, the criminally insane, and third-party presidential candidates.[10]

10. Yes, I realize this is redundant.

Social Revolutions

The social revolution is one of the more common, but gradual of the revolutions. The Civil Rights Movement and the Counterculture Revolution of the Sixties are all examples of social revolutions. When most people say, "We want a social revolution," what they really mean to say is, "We want to start a bottom-up social uprising in an attempt at reforming society's attitudes towards religion, personal identity, and freedom of speech." Unfortunately, this does not fit on a bumper sticker[11] — and if it's not on a bumper sticker, it doesn't exist.

11. Unless you drive a Hummer.

Proletarian/Communist Revolutions

A proletarian revolution or "communist revolution," as it is known to those who enjoy wearing lots of red, is the name given to a revolution in which the working class overthrows capitalism. The proletarian revolution is the cornerstone of Marxism, and is favored by those who can't afford the more expensive, shinier revolutions.

Non-Violent Revolutions

A centuries old idea, the non-violent revolution became popular with Mahatma Gandhi and Martin Luther King Jr. Most non-violent revolutions are named after fruits, flowers, or candy,[12] such as Ukraine's Orange Revolution, the Republic of Kyrgyzstan's Tulip Revolution, and Georgia's Rose Revolution. This strikes fear into the hearts of anyone who fears fruits or flowers. Non-violent revolutions generally tend to be boring.

12. Such as the Lichtenstein Marzipan Revolution.

INTELLECTUAL/PHILOSPHICAL/ TECHNOLOGICAL REVOLUTIONS

Agricultural Revolutions

The agricultural revolution is a type of revolution in which advancements in technology lead to increases in agricultural productivity. It's also the name given to any revolution where farmers attempt to overthrow oppressive ears of corn.[13]

13. And celery, if it's in season.

Digital Revolutions

The original digital revolution, which saw the birth of the personal computer, lasted from 1834 to 1835. This revolution quickly waned however, once it became clear that computers would serve no practical purpose. The computer has since been replaced by the more practical abacus.

Industrial Revolutions

The industrial revolution was a period during the 18th and 19th centuries in Britain, and later the rest of the world, that brought about the origination of machinery and steam power. These advancements have since fundamentally changed nearly all aspects of our lives. When you wake up in the morning for work, look at your steam-powered alarm clock and think, "If it weren't for the industrial revolution, I'd still be asleep right now."

Scientific Revolutions

See: Proletarian/Communist Revolutions, but with scientists.

Sexual Revolutions

A sexual revolution is generally anything that Madonna did in the '80s.[14] Considered by historians to be one of the more enjoyable revolutions, the number of sexual revolutions throughout history far outweighs the number of non-sexual revolutions. If you're allowed just one revolution in your lifetime, make it a sexual revolution.[15]

14. Except vogueing.

15. And if you're allowed just one beer, make it a Bud Light.

MISCELLANEOUS REVOLUTIONS

The Singing Revolution

These are the revolutions that led to the independence of Estonia, Latvia, and Lithuania. They were also one of the few revolutions to have been written by Rodgers & Hammerstein.

The Quiet Revolution

This is the revolutionary name given to a period of social change, which occurred in Quebec, Canada in the 1960s. This revolution is also preferable if the baby is sleeping.

The Dance Dance Revolution

A symbolic period in history, in which youth across America rose up together to fight against their feudalistic noble oppressors by stepping forward, backward, backward, right, left, right, right, forward, backward, left, backward.

The Matrix Revolutions

Keanu Reeves led this important revolution, which would later turn out to be the more boring in a trilogy of three revolutions about philosophy and dodging bullets. This revolution was written by the Wachowski Brothers.

The New England Revolution

This is a soccer team. So in other words, this revolution doesn't apply to the United States.

Revolution Pet Medicine

Give to your dog or cat once a month in order to prevent heartworms, fleas, ear mites, and scabies.

Don't see your favorite brand of revolution listed here? Feel free to add your own in the space provided:

_____

_____

_____

_____

_____

A REVOLUTIONARY FUN FACT!

In some communist countries, it is illegal to revolt against the government.

COUNTRIES AND THEIR REVOLUTIONS

Nearly all modern countries have had to go through some growing pains. In order to become a successful and mature nation, a country must first suffer through puberty, be made fun of in gym class, awkwardly make out with its date at the prom, and survive through a political revolution. Only after experiencing these growing pains[16] can an awkward and pimple-faced country become a superpower.

The following are some of the more significant revolutions of the most powerful countries in the world, and Canada, arranged in no particular order.

Aside from alphabetical.

16. Don't forget the embarrassing coup d'état!

BELGIUM

Revolution: Belgian Revolution

Years: 1830

Revolutionary:
Erasme Louis Surlet de Chokier

Result: The establishment of an independent and neutral Belgium

A Belgian revolution, covered in strawberries and topped with powdered sugar, is one of the more popular items at IHOP.

BRAZIL

Revolution: Brazilian Declaration of Independence

Years: 1821

Revolutionary: Brazilian Revolutionaries

Result: Independence of Brazil

The obvious byproduct of the Brazilian Declaration of Independence was the eventual independence of Brazil. The less obvious byproduct of the Brazilian Declaration of Independence is a country full of very attractive people.

CANADA

Revolution: Never experienced its own revolution

Years: N/A

Revolutionary: No one.

Result: No result.

Nothing has ever happened in Canada.

CHINA

Revolution: Cultural Revolution

Years: 1966-1968

Revolutionary: Mao Zedong

Result: The death of opposing party leaders

Contrary to popular belief, the cultural revolution didn't involve '"culture" as much as it involved "killing intellectuals." But let's not nitpick.

FRANCE

Revolution: French Revolution
Years: 1789-1799
Revolutionary:
Several French Revolutionaries
Result: Various forms of government

The downside of the French Revolution is that France went through various forms of government during a span of several decades. The upside of the French Revolution is that it was the only revolution to come with its own wine pairing.

INDIA

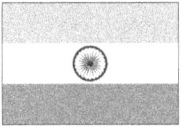

Revolution: White Revolution
Years: 1970
Revolutionary:
National Dairy Development Board
Result: A nationwide milk grid

Some people have argued that a revolution can't involve milk. India proved that not only can milk inspire a revolution, but that a warm glass of milk can also help soothe an upset stomach.

NETHERLANDS

Revolution: Dutch Revolution
Years: 1568-1648
Revolutionary: William of Orange
Result: The rise of the Dutch Republic as a major power

One of only two revolutions to have been fought while wearing small wooden clogs.

RUSSIA

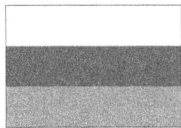

Revolution: October Revolution
Years: 1917
Revolutionary: Vladimir Lenin
Result: Power given to the Soviets

Historians are unsure when the October Revolution is to have occurred, but a general consensus is sometime in the spring.

SPAIN

Revolution: Glorious Revolution
Years: 1868
Revolutionary: Eddie Izzard
Result: Overthrow of King James II of England

Also sometimes known as the "Spectacular Revolution," the "Outstanding Revolution," and the "Are You Kidding Me, These Tapas Are Amazing Revolution."

UNITED STATES

Revolution: American Revolution
Years: 1773-1775
Revolutionary: George Washington
Result: United States

A turning point in U.S. history, marked every year with celebrations, parades, and furniture sales.

? A REVOLUTIONARY QUIZ ?

If you were a revolutionary, you would prefer to spend your time in:

A) The United States, while in the midst of the American Revolution. You love freedom!

B) Russia, during the time of the Bolshevik Revolution. October is your favorite month!

C) France, throughout the French Revolution. Thank you Age of Enlightenment, for Democracy!

D) Revolution Land: a subsidiary of Six Flags Amusement Parks. Half-price admission for those dressed up as Vladimir Lenin — or by bringing in a Coke can!

FAMOUS REVOLUTIONARIES

If I were to say, "Name a famous revolutionary," you would probably ask, "What's in it for me?" After I offered you a free coupon to Applebee's, you would probably say, "Che Guevara." Some revolutionaries are famous and instantly come to mind. Most people, for example, have heard of George Washington. There are very few people who don't know who Joan of Arc is. Who doesn't know the story behind Chairman Mao? Nearly everyone has heard of Malcolm X, and those who haven't should go back to school (to see if their school offers a tuition refund[17]). Nevertheless, what many people don't realize is that not all revolutionaries have been involved in battle or in large political causes.

Some revolutionaries have changed the world through their own small changes and discoveries. If it weren't for Thomas Edison, you would be reading this book by candlelight. If it weren't for Chef Boyardee, a lot of college students would not have had breakfast this morning. If it weren't for eHarmony, many people would not have discovered how easy it is to Photoshop one's own picture. Revolutionaries come in all shapes and sizes, and unlike Mahatma Gandhi, not all of them carry guns. By simply changing the course of humanity, one becomes a revolutionary.[18]

But I'm not going to discuss them. If I were to list the name of every person who's ever altered the course of history, the list would stretch from here until probably a few miles from here. It's really hard to know though, because no one's ever actually made such a list. The length of such a

17. Sometimes the University of Phoenix will offer a 30-day policy.

18. Well, after a lengthy application.

list is purely conjecture — and poor conjecture at that.

This list will provide you with the names of revolutionaries that everyone usually learns in school. You can probably skip this part.

IN THEIR OWN REVOLUTIONARY WORDS

"Every generation needs a new revolution. Every rose has its thorn."

THOMAS JEFFERSON
U.S. President and Revolutionary

REVOLUTIONARIES
YOU SHOULD KNOW

Abbie Hoffman

A political activist who co-founded the Youth International Party, he came into the national spotlight for being arrested as one of the "Chicago Eight,"[19] a group of eight men charged with conspiracy during the riots of the 1968 Democratic National Convention. He would later declare bankruptcy, since many people read the title of his 1971 book, *Steal This Book*, and then did.

19. Not to be confused with the Jackson Five.

The Beatles

A groundbreaking rock group formed in the early 1960s; The Beatles were one of the most commercially successful bands of all time, as well as one of the most revolutionary. Having found success early in their career, The Beatles would later turn their attentions to social awareness, including the hit song "Revolution." Not entirely clear on the purpose of the revolution, most people simply got stoned and listened to "Revolution."

Che Guevara

A guerilla leader and iconic Argentine revolutionary, he played a large role in the Cuban Revolution. After his 1967 execution by the Bolivian army, he later went on to make a line of T-shirts and mugs with his face on them.[20]

20. Available at Wal-Mart.

Francisco Madero

The leading revolutionary in the Mexican Revolution, Francisco Madero also served as Mexico's president from 1911 to 1913. An avid vegetarian, he was assassinated after he was betrayed by Victoriano Huerta over a dispute regarding tofurkey. It is from his death that we get the proverb "A vegetarian Mexican president cannot pass through the eye of a needle to enter the kingdom of God, and will therefore be assassinated."[21]

21. Matthew 19:24, in one of the more modern versions.

Francois-Marie Arouet de Voltaire

A French writer, philosopher, and polemicist whose writings about social and political reform would later influence other revolutionaries such as Thomas Paine. He would eventually come to be known by the pen name of "Voltaire," since "Francois-Marie Arouet de" was way too faggy.[22]

22. If you think the word "faggy" is offensive, you should hear some of the other words Voltaire was called in gym class.

Frederick Douglass

One of the most influential abolitionists and orators of the 19th century, he played a major part in the eventual freedom of African-Americans. Douglass was known by many nicknames through his life, including, "The Lion of Anacostia." This is because he once caught and devoured a gazelle with his bare hands.

George Washington

The first American president and one of the original founding fathers, George Washington is considered the quintessential American revolutionary. While the belief that he wore wooden teeth is simply a myth, the belief that his entire sternum was made of plastic is absolutely true.

Georges Danton

23. He had been promoted from Hall Monitor.

He was one of the leading revolutionaries in the French Revolution, as well as the first president of the Committee of Public Safety.[23] Realizing that he would be remembered in history for something as dull as "president of a safety committee," he agreed to be decapitated.

Gloria Steinem

One of the nation's most iconic feminists, Ms. Steinem founded the feminist magazine *Ms.* in 1972. She chose the name "Ms." as the title of her magazine after rejecting other suggested titles, including "Miss.," "Mrs.," and "You Can Call Me Whatever You Want, As Long As I Get Home In Time to Make Supper For My Husband."

Ho Chi Minh

A revolutionary and eventual president of North Vietnam, he led the Vietminh against the Japanese during World War II. Ho Chi Minh City, the largest city in Vietnam, is proof that all revolutionaries will get a city named after them.[24]

24. This is how the city of Margaritaville was founded.

Jesus Christ

Amongst his teachings were the laws of "loving God," "loving thy neighbor," and "hating people who are pro-choice and pro-gun control laws." In addition to encouraging the idea of non-violent revolutions, he would later become famous for having discovered the concept of Christianity. This fact has since been disputed, as some historians believe that he may have stolen this concept from another well-known philosopher of the time, Bob Christ.[25]

25. No relation.

Joan of Arc

In an attempt at padding her college entrance application, Joan of Arc commanded the entire French army at the age of seventeen in 1429. She was burned at the stake two years later, and consequently did not attend college.

John Hancock

A revolutionary who became the first governor of Massachusetts, as well as one of the founding fathers, he is best remembered as having been the first person to sign the Declaration of Independence. Which is a good thing, for the second person to sign was Zebediah Asfrynkthpbbbbtlzinskiro.[26]

Joseph Stalin

History is unsure how to best remember Joseph Stalin, who became the General Secretary of the Communist Party of the Soviet Union's Central Committee. On the negative side, his dictatorship and campaigns of political repression killed millions of people. On the positive side, the Soviet Union played a large role in defeating Nazi Germany under his leadership. On the negative side, he had a habit of slapping babies. On the positive side, he was the co-founder of the Disney channel.

Karl Marx

A writer, philosopher, and revolutionary, he is often referred to as the "Father of Communism." He is best known for his 1848 bestseller, *Communist Manifesto*, which he later followed with the bestselling sequel, *Sex, Lies, and Videotape: Sharing Your Possessions With Your Neighbors.*[27]

Mahatma Gandhi

An iconic spiritual and political leader in India during the 1940s, he is best remembered for his advocacy of non-violence and vegetarianism. It has since been discovered that Gandhi's vegetarianism wasn't as much a path to spiritual enlightenment, as much as it was because he thought he was fat and wanted to lose a few pounds.

Malcolm X

A political activist, he advocated the use of violence in his campaign for black equality, only to be assassinated in 1965. He was preceded by Malcolms I through IX.

Napoleon Bonaparte

Eventually becoming the Emperor of France, he began his career as a general in the French Revolution. He united France, but was later captured by the British and imprisoned until his death on the island of Saint Helena. Famous for having a height of only 5'2", he paved the way for other revolutionaries of short stature, including Danny DeVito.

Thomas Paine

He was a revolutionary and political writer whose 1776 pamphlet, *Common Sense*, called for American independence. Fearful that he would be remembered by history as simply "that guy who wrote a pamphlet," he would later go on to hold the world record for "world's longest fingernails."

William Wallace

He led the resistance during the Wars of Scottish Independence, which would later become the inspiration behind the film *Braveheart*. He also went on to direct and produce the film *The Passion of the Christ*, as well as star in *What Women Want*.[28]

28. Little known revolutionary fact: He is also the only Scottish revolutionary to win an Academy Award, while simultaneously being anti-Semitic.

? A REVOLUTIONARY QUIZ ?

You consider one of the most successful revolutionaries in history to be:

A) Martin Luther King Jr. — for his fundamental role in promoting equal civil rights for all Americans.

B) Che Guevara — for his role as "supreme prosecutor" and Marxist revolutionary.

C) Jesus Christ — for pioneering the peaceful protest and paving the way for eternal salvation.

D) LuEsther Mertz — for founding the company Publisher's Clearing House. Thanks to LuEsther, direct marketing sweepstakes no longer have to live in slavery, partly due to the valiant efforts of the company's militant wing, the Prize Patrol.

REVOLUTIONARIES YOU DON'T NEED TO WORRY ABOUT

- Joseph McCarthy
- Lyndon LaRouche
- Emo Kids
- The Atkins Diet
- L. Ron Hubbard
- Skinny Jeans
- The Internet
- Ron Paul
- The Ginsu Knife

MODERN REVOLUTIONS

Historical revolutions are great, but they're also … what's the word I'm looking for … really historic. Which is a polite way of saying really old. In fact, if you refer to an elderly person as "really historic," they absolutely will not take offense.[29]

29. At least that's what Larry King told me.

While historical revolutions have had their day in the sun, a shinier, newer model is always preferred. No one wants a black and white television when a plasma flat screen is available. No one wants a rotary phone when an iPhone is on sale. No one wants a Sega Genesis when a Nintendo Wii can be purchased. No one wants to flip a light switch when The Clapper is kind of a good substitute.

The same idea applies to revolutions. Karl Marx may have been the revolutionary behind Communism a century and a half ago, but his chunky ankles most likely wouldn't

30. Shoe size
9 ½ .

fit into the stilettos of Miss Sylvia Rivera,[30] the drag queen who incited the Stonewall Riots of the late 1960s. The revolutions and movements of yesterday have been replaced with the revolutions and movements of today, allowing humanity to progress. However, I wouldn't suggest that you become too comfortable with the revolutions and movements of today, because like iPods or trophy wives, a newer and better one is always right around the corner.

Looking for your own revolution to join? Might I suggest one of the following modern movements, now in progress:

Women's Rights Movement

Could a woman be president? I wouldn't know, because I don't follow the news (Ross Perot was re-elected, right?). Nevertheless, the fact that a woman may or may not someday become president doesn't automatically forgive thousands, if not dozens of years of female repression. In some parts of Alabama, women still aren't allowed to vote, in other parts of Kentucky women still aren't allowed to drive, and in a few backwards parts of California, women still aren't allowed to vote and drive at the same time. Do we, as a modern society, accept this inequality? Men are allowed to drive and vote at the same time, whereas women aren't even allowed to arrange a babysitter? If you're looking for a modern revolution, the women's rights movement needs you.

Civil Rights Movement

While the Civil Rights movement saw its peak during the '50s, the ' 60s, as well as anytime the Reverend Al

Sharpton opens his mouth, the struggle for equality continues even to this day. Despite the fact that we've had a black president, black people are still not allowed to partake in certain aspects of society, which many white people take for granted. Only white people are allowed to listen to awful country music. Only white people are allowed to not know how to dance. Only white people were allowed to be Michael Jackson. What's next, only white people will be allowed to join the NAACP? We will not stand for this injustice! If you're looking for a modern revolution, the civil rights movement needs you.

Gay Rights Movement

They're here, they're queer, and they'll finish the rest of the chant once the legislation passes. Can you imagine having to ask permission for everything you do — and then waiting for politicians to give their approval? "Excuse me sir, do you mind if I not be fired from my job?" Ridiculous! Being gay means you're not allowed to get gay married, you're not allowed to hold down a gay job, and you're not even allowed to audition for American Idol. Sometimes it seems as though the only thing gay people are allowed to do is be gay — and where's the fun in that?[31] If you're looking for a modern revolution, the gay rights movement needs you.

31. Other than the great clothes and looking fabulous.

Immigrants' Rights Movement

Some people complain that they want illegal immigrants to return to their own country. Does this make sense? Has anyone stopped to think that if no one picks the lettuce, then the lettuce will pick us? Illegal immigrants are the backbone of our great country and nothing should take that away, with the exception of osteoporosis. If society loses illegal immigrants, it will be only a matter of time before we lose legal immigrants. If we lose legal immigrants, it won't be long before we lose the legal system. And if we lose the legal system, Nancy Grace will be out of a job. Look at who we've become — we're picking lettuce ourselves, and we've caused Nancy Grace's unemployment. If you're looking for a modern revolution, the immigrants' rights movement needs you.

Human Rights Movement

I don't understand what the big deal is when it comes to torture. My brothers teased and tortured me when I was young, and my scars didn't turn out that bad.[32] In fact, it's surprising how quickly I can forget that I was tortured with a cattle prod as a child. Despite my own enjoyable experiences with waterboarding, I recognize that some people believe it should be "illegal" to torture. "But what about human rights?" they ask. "Not everyone enjoys being deprived of sleep for seventy-two hours while simultaneously being attacked by a German Shepherd!" they complain. I have to concede that they have a point. In the name of human rights, no one "should" have to be tortured — against their will. If you're looking for a modern revolution, the human rights movement needs you.

32. If I hold perfectly still, you totally can't tell that my left eyeball has been punctured with a curling iron.

A REVOLUTIONARY FUN FACT!

Carl McGovern, April 17, 1846.

2 media: killing us softly with their song

Congratulations, you've just created the tastiest hamburger in the tri-state area. Like anyone who has ever created a tasty burger, you wish to mass-produce it and market it to the world. Sure, it's dripping with additives and has enough saturated fat to kill a horse, but that's beside the point. You've spent hours upon minutes perfecting the recipe,[33] and shouldn't the world know about this gastronomical wonder?

The same thing is true for a revolution. You have the Next Big Idea that will change the world. Communism?

33. Which, ironically, is made of horsemeat.

Respect for women? Fairer wages? Wanna throw tea into the harbor? The goal of your revolution doesn't matter. What does matter though, is how you market your revolution. Marketing your revolution is the first big step in letting the world know about your revolution. It's important that other people know about your passionate uprising. After all, you're so angry, you could just spit! Unless you're in Singapore, in which case you'll be arrested.

Learning about past revolutions in print media, music, and television will give you a better idea of how to market your own societal upheaval. You've created the tastiest hamburger ever — share it with the world! You've created the best revolution — share it with the world! Either way, you'll be competing with McDonald's.

IN THEIR OWN REVOLUTIONARY WORDS

"When Liberty comes with hands dabbled in blood it is hard to shake hands with her. You know what's also gross? People who don't wash their hands after using the bathroom."

OSCAR WILDE
Irish Playwright and author

REVOLUTIONS IN PRINT MEDIA

All revolutions begin with the printed word. Before the days of fancy television commercials for political uprisings and musical jingles for shampoo,[34] existed the poor

34. Both owned by Procter & Gamble.

peasant boy. These peasant boys would distribute pamphlets across the village for a shilling, and then take that shilling to the neighborhood nickelodeon to watch a Punch and Judy show while gorging himself on sweets. The poor peasant boy wasn't very bright, and it really doesn't make sense why anyone would trust him with pamphlets in the first place.

Before you say to yourself, "I'm going to make a boring documentary about my political cause," you need to ask yourself, "But what about a pamphlet?" Centuries of manipulative propaganda have existed in which something as simple as a poster or a pamphlet has motivated multitudes of people. Before entertaining other options, ask yourself, "Would a pamphlet have the same effect?"

The answer to this is usually "no." Stick to the documentary.

The following is a glossary of terms that you will need to know if you wish to employ the print media in your own revolution.

Propaganda

35. Little known revolutionary fact: Dick Clark used to protest against the Vietnam War in the early '70s by writing protest messages on the confetti strips in Times Square during New Year's Eve.

This is the broad term we give to anything that promotes a political or religious idea or belief. Propaganda can cover anything, ranging from posters and pamphlets, to business cards and confetti. It's worth pointing out that confetti can convey a lot more information than most people realize, and can be used anywhere from New Years Eve parties to ticker-tape parades.[35] A good rule of thumb to remember is that if the propaganda comes from your own revolution, it's the truth and generally good. If it comes from someone else's revolution, it's all lies and generally bad.

Pamphleteer

The Pamphleteer is the pawn of the revolution.[36] They don't do much fighting, they hardly inspire anyone, and all they do is sit around writing pamphlets all day in their pajamas. Years later, the pamphleteer will choose to go by another name, that of "blogger." Before the celebrity blog, there existed "Ye Olde Celebrity Gossip Pamphlet." Despite their purposelessness, the pamphleteer will occasionally play an important part in a revolution, although this part usually consists of making a Starbucks run to get coffee for everyone else.

36. Ironically, they're very bad at chess.

Pamphlet

The dissemination of the revolution originally came from this — the humble pamphlet. Small in stature and low in voltage, the pamphlet was able to carry a wallop of information. "Come Join the Communist Party — Everybody's Doing it! And You'll Be Killed If You Don't!" was a popular pamphlet title, for example. These pamphlets would be distributed by peasant boys everywhere — pubs, churches, strip joints, factories, and paper shredders. While the pamphlet is an antiquated idea and is hardly used at all anymore, it is always an option for the revolutionary who is short on money but has an excess of peasant boys.

Protest Signs

Before the protest sign, revolutionaries for years protested in front of their factories, chanting and holding up nothing more than a bare post. Realizing this was ineffective, it was later decided that a "sign" should be attached to the bare post, thus giving birth to the protest sign. A staple of any modern protest or strike, the protest sign usually consists of a catchy phrase in neon colors. While it's not necessary that the phrase rhyme, I cannot stress enough the importance of using a pun. A protest sign without a pun is like a baby without a head — absolutely worthless. Using a pun drives home the point of the revolution, as well as providing amusement for passersby. If I drive by and see, "We Want the Truth," I won't bat an eye. If I drive by and see, "Prevent Truth Decay," I will actually quit my job and join that revolution.

Tabloids

Most people don't consider the common tabloid to be a source of propaganda. Most people also don't consider Crosby, Stills & Nash to be a better band without Neil Young. In both cases, these people would be wrong.[37] The tabloid is one of the most effective, potent tools a revolutionary has at their disposal. Ask anyone on the street which starlet-of-the-week is currently in rehab, and they will tell you. Tabloids reach everyone and better yet, people assume they're true. Chairman Mao's rise to power? Salacious gossip written about him in the tabloids. How did Joseph Stalin lead the

37. If you don't believe me, ask your parents. Or Neil Young.

Soviet Union to become the world's second largest super-power? The National Inquirer accused him of being gay.[38] Consider taking up a job as a paparazzo (tell friends you're becoming a "photojournalist" if you're embarrassed). Take embarrassing pictures of rival revolutionaries in compromising situations. It will do wonders for your movement.

38. The sex tape didn't help.

A REVOLUTIONARY DO-IT-YOURSELF PAMPHLET

Let's face it — the modern revolutionary is busier than ever. Between organizing strikes, sticking it to the man, and attending your child's PTA meeting, you just don't have the time to both design and distribute your own manipulative propaganda pamphlet. For that reason, I've come up with the do-it-yourself pamphlet. Simply follow these steps, and you have your own pamphlet, ready for distribution. ➡

Front Cover

1. Choose an image. Any of the following images are effective:

- An animal. The more fangs, the better, but limit the number of tails to four.
- An oil tanker on fire.
- A picture of your opponent, but without a head and/or genitals. Swapping head for genitals is also accepted.
- A kitten. But only if it's coated in blood (not its own) and draped in a flag with Communist symbols.

2. Come up with a good title for your pamphlet. It's preferable that the title be really sarcastic and condescending, like Thomas Paine's "Common Sense." The following is a list of possible sarcastic pamphlet names, free for your use.

- "Stop Reading This Pamphlet Or You'll Miss the Short Bus"
- "Everything in this Pamphlet Is Important"
- "All of the Political Theories Within this Pamphlet are Far too Advanced for Your Understanding, So Don't Even Bother"
- "Common Sense, 2"

Everything in this pamphlet is important

Contents of the Pamphlet

1. Check out *Writing Revolutionary Pamphlets for Dummies*[39] from your local library. Be sure to pay attention to chapters 3, 4, and 12. You'll also want to check out the cartoons by Rich Tennant, because they're really funny.

39. Never mind, someone just barely checked it out.

Back Cover

"The Holocaust was an obscene period in our nation's history. I mean in this century's history. But we all lived in this century. I didn't live in this century."

— Dan Quayle

1. Get a quote for the back from someone famous, like Frederick Douglass or Dan Quayle.

2. You will need a really classy picture of yourself for the author photo. I strongly suggest taking the picture at a Glamour Shots studio, usually located in your local mall. If there is not a Glamour Shots studio in your local mall, due to the fact that you currently do not live in the 1980s, a camera phone held up to a mirror will suffice.[40]

40. Don't forget to wear your Che Guevara T-shirt in the picture!

I should also point out that any pamphlet longer than ten pages automatically becomes a manifesto. If you're going to write a manifesto, you may as well grow out your beard, claim you're the Messiah, move out to a cabin in the woods, and threaten to blow people up. Otherwise, keep your pamphlet to less than ten pages.

2. While the content of your pamphlet depends entirely on the type of revolution in which you are engaged, it's generally a good rule of thumb that the pamphlet not extend more than ten pages. It's well known that all revolutionaries have notoriously short attention spans.

A WARNING ABOUT "PROPAGANDA"

Like "baby killer" or "I'm sleeping with your brother," the word "propaganda" has gotten a bad rap over the years. For some reason, many people — both revolutionaries and non-revolutionaries — associate the word with manipulating a group of people to perform evil deeds. Not only is this unfair to the word "propaganda," but it completely ignores the fact that there are other, more inappropriate words that convince people to do evil. Such as, for example, "alcohol."

It is well known that Adolf Hitler used propaganda to convince German citizens about the benefits of Nazism, and as both history and statistics later proved, Hitler wasn't a moral person. Statistically speaking. Hitler wasn't alone, as other dictators also used propaganda to manipulate the masses, including Benito Mussolini, Joseph Stalin, and Walt Disney.

When using literature, music, television, or film to encourage others to join your revolution, it is important to avoid the word "propaganda" at all costs. Use a more consumer-friendly word, such as "manipulation tool" or "sacrificial revolutionary recruiter."

REVOLUTIONS IN MUSIC

Every war, every fight, and every movement has had its own inspirational musical soundtrack. To be fair, most of the time this music is terrible, and blasting it from communal loudspeakers only makes a bad situation worse. Nevertheless, an inspirational song — whether it be Woody Guthrie's "This Land Is Your Land" or Destiny's Child's "Bootylicious" — can still inspire a revolution.

When determining a song to use for one's revolution, the following questions must be asked: Does it have a good beat? Does it have lyrics that can easily be chanted? Does it have at least one stanza that can fit on a placard and be carried around? Is the song written or sung by Jimmy Buffett? These questions are essential, because more than one revolution has used a song by Jimmy Buffett.[41] This is only appropriate if the revolution happens to occur on a cruise ship, and all revolutionaries involved are drinking margaritas and over the age of 50.

The following is a brief list of the countless number of revolutionary and protest songs, which will inspire you to choose one of your own. You may be curious as to why this list begins with songs from the Cold War. This is primarily because revolutionary music was invented in 1960. Prior to this time, only three revolutionary songs existed: "La Marseillaise," which doesn't count because it is in French; "Yankee Doodle Dandy," which has been banned in most states due to its profanity; and "Battle Hymn of the Republic," which is now only sung at Easter under federal law.

41. This will not be the last time "Margaritaville" is referenced in this book. You're welcome.

"LONDON CALLING" BY THE CLASH

This song from the 1979 album of the same name, was inspired by the melt-down of a nuclear reactor at Three Mile Island, which had occurred only nine months before. Because Three Mile Island is located in Pennsylvania,[42] and telephones hadn't been invented yet in 1979, the title, "London Calling," makes absolutely no sense.

"99 LUFTBALLONS" BY NENA

Originally recorded in German in the early Eighties only to later be re-recorded in English as "99 Red Balloons," this song tells the tale of balloons floating over the Berlin Wall during the Cold War. U.S. President Jimmy Carter reportedly hated it, due to his irrational fear of German balloons.[43]

"RUSSIANS" BY STING

A song from Sting's 1985 debut album, The Dream of the Blue Turtles, "Russians" weaves a cautionary tale about the repercussions of the Cold War. A small con-troversy erupted later that year however, when it was discovered that the song "Russians" came with a complimentary bottle of vodka.[44]

"BORN IN THE U.S.A." BY BRUCE SPRINGSTEEN

This song by Bruce Springsteen, from the critically acclaimed album of the same name, was written as a tribute to the hardships his friends experienced after hav-ing returned from the Vietnam War. Ironically, this song was made in China.

"BLOWIN' IN THE WIND" BY BOB DYLAN

An incredibly versatile song, Bob Dylan's quintessential protest song of the 1960s has been used in protest against everything from the Vietnam War to the Iraq War. It also works well in commercials, selling everything from Cadillacs to soup.

"THE UNKNOWN SOLDIER" BY THE DOORS

From the 1968 album Waiting for the Sun, this song was Jim Morrison's reaction to the Vietnam War. Upon the revelation of newly discovered birth certificates, the name of the song was changed from "The Unknown Soldier" to "Bob Stevenson of Trenton, New Jersey."

42. It's now a resort and spa. You should visit sometime.
43. Also, spiders. To this day, he refuses to watch the film Arachnophobia in German subtitles.
44. Vermouth sold separately.

"STREETS OF SORROW/BIRMINGHAM SIX" BY THE POGUES

A political song from The Pogues' 1988 album, *If I Should Fall From Grace*; it describes the pain felt at the height of The Troubles. As for the actual name of the song, it is taken from the address of The Pogues' former studio, located on the corner of Streets of Sorrow and Birmingham Six. Go down Melancholy Avenue and turn left. If you run into Desolation Boulevard, you've gone too far.

"SUNDAY BLOODY SUNDAY" BY U2

Considering that U2 hailed from Ireland, it only makes sense that the band would eventually write a song describing the horror felt by an observer of The Troubles in Northern Ireland. In particular, this song references the Bloody Sunday incident in Derry. What many people don't realize is that this song is the reason there are only six days in the week.[45]

"ZOMBIE" BY THE CRANBERRIES

One of The Cranberries' most successful songs ever, it comes from their 1994 album, *No Need to Argue*. The song, which laments The Troubles in Northern Ireland, is a particular reference to a deadly werewolf attack in Dublin in 1983.

"AMERICAN IDIOT" BY GREEN DAY

From the Grammy Award winning album of the same name, comes this song that criticizes the propaganda and paranoia of a post-9/11 United States. The title of the song also behaves as an international insult, regardless of where you are in the world. You can offend an American by calling him an "idiot," and you can offend anyone else in the world by calling him an "American."[46]

"LET'S IMPEACH THE PRESIDENT" BY NEIL YOUNG

A Grammy Award nominated protest song, this is from the 2006 album, *Living with War*. It is sung to the tune of Steve Goodman's song, "The City of New Orleans." This also happens to be one of the very few songs in history to resign before being impeached by Congress.

"DEAR MR. PRESIDENT" BY PINK

This popular song by Pink and featuring the Indigo Girls, is an open letter to former President of the United States, George W. Bush. The song addresses such issues as the Iraq War, homosexuality, the homeless, abortion, and drug abuse. Pink continued these themes two years later in a follow up song titled, "Dear Santa Claus."

45. And on the sixth day, U2 rested.
46. Unless you're Canadian.

"SAY IT LOUD — I'M BLACK AND PROUD" BY JAMES BROWN
Recorded in 1968, this song soon became one of the most popular "black pow-er" anthems of the 1960s. The song would later become so well known over the years that a number of different black artists covered it; the most famous version was sung by Garth Brooks.

"I AM WOMAN" BY HELEN REDDY
This song, released in 1972, eventually became known as the iconic anthem of the women's rights movement. It later received the Grammy for "Song Most Used By Drag Queens Everywhere."[47]

"WE SHALL OVERCOME" BY REVEREND CHARLES TINDLEY
One of the most well known protest and revolutionary songs of the past cen-tury, this 1947 song eventually became the key anthem of the U.S. Civil Rights movement. In the past 50 years, this song has reached a level of such somber respect, that it has become a favorite among American Idol contestants.[48]

"GIVE PEACE A CHANCE" BY JOHN LENNON
This well-known song was recorded by Lennon during his famous bed-in with Yoko Ono in 1969. Many people are surprised to learn though that Lennon killed two people in the process of writing the lyrics.

"IMAGINE" BY JOHN LENNON
This powerful song which was released in 1971, was described by Lennon as being "an anti-religious, anti-nationalistic, anti-conventional, anti-capitalistic song." Two years later, he sold the rights of the song to the Catholic Church to use in McDonald's commercials on the Fourth of July.

"HEAL THE WORLD" BY MICHAEL JACKSON
From the album *Dangerous* comes this song which illustrates Jackson's desire to make the world a better and safer place. It is also known for its performance during the Super Bowl XXVII halftime show in 1993, which featured a 35,000 person flash card performance. To prove his dedication to the message of healing the world, Jackson went so far as to be accused of pedophilia two years later.[49]

47. It barely beat out *It's Raining Men*.
48. Especially during "Disco Week."
49. Too soon?

"POWER TO THE PEOPLE" BY JOHN LENNON

Recorded with the Plastic Ono Band, this was Lennon's attempt at penning an anthem for the protests occurring at the time. Journalist Hunter S. Thompson criticized the song however, saying it was "ten years too late." It is important to point out that Thompson was stoned at the time. It is also likely that Lennon was stoned when he wrote the song. In fact, most people reading this book will be surprised to learn that they too are stoned.

"ROCK THE CASBAH" BY THE CLASH

Not many songs can claim to have been inspired by the banning of rock music in Iran under Ayatollah Khomeini, but The Clash was no ordinary band. This song from the album *Combat Rock* is one of only two songs to have let that raga drop.

"WHAT'S GOING ON?" BY MARVIN GAYE

From his 1971 album of the same name, this song addressed political and social troubles in the world, as well as black-on-black crime. The sexy song is also known for seducing a number of married women.

CHOOSING YOUR OWN REVOLUTIONARY SONG

It's very common for the budding revolutionary to wish to write his or her own revolutionary song. And why not? A successful song can bring with it the possibility of fame and success, a Grammy award,[50] jewels and fur coats, and bitches and hoes. Understandably, the allure of writing one's own revolutionary song can be far too tantalizing to pass up.

50. Although let's be honest, anyone with $15 and a pulse can get a Grammy award.

Do not give in to temptation!

Instructing you not to write your own revolutionary song may seem confusing and counter intuitive at first, for up to this point I've encouraged you, the reader, to take a hands-on approach to your revolution. Nevertheless, song writing is not

51. As
opposed
to a round
of baccarat,
which is *always*
necessary.

a feat to be taken on by amateurs. Revolutionary songs are not children's playthings. Not only is writing one's own revolutionary song dangerous, but it is also highly unnecessary.[51]

To write such a song requires dedication, a musical degree from a serious college, and a healthy dose of moxie and/or gumption. These are not traits found in the average revolutionary. Have you ever wondered why Martin Luther King Jr. never wrote his own revolutionary songs? What about Ho Chi Minh, where are his chart-toppers? This isn't an accident. This is because revolutionaries *do not write songs*. Well, except for John Lennon.[52]

For this reason, I shared the list of historical revolutionary songs on the previous pages. I cannot tell you which song will be most appropriate for your revolution, but I can advise that you keep the following four questions in mind, when choosing a song from the vast library of protest and revolutionary songs available:

Rhythm. Does it have a good rhythm?

Beat. Does it have a good beat?

Lyrics. Does it have good lyrics?

Frequency. What's the frequency, Kenneth?[53]

REVOLUTIONS IN TELEVISION

If a picture is worth a thousand words, and a Coke is worth $1.49, then revolutions must have a long history intertwined with television. Don't believe me? Haven't you ever wondered why, whenever Jack Tripper burst through the door on the television show *Three's Company*, he had

A REVOLUTIONARY QUIZ

If you had to choose a song to symbolize your own revolution, it would be:

A) "Imagine" — The lyrics alone inspire humankind to wish for a peaceful utopia.

B) "We Shall Overcome" — This anthem, when set against a background of civil disobedience, encourages unity and brotherhood.

C) "I Am Woman" — A song which motivates women everywhere to stand up with one voice and demand equal rights.

D) "Who Put the Bomp In the Bomp-a-Bomp-a-Bomp?" — No, seriously, I want to know who put the ram in the ram-a-lam-a-ding-dong?

a bayonet in one hand and a flag which read "Liberté, Égalité, Fraternité" in the other? It's clearly because *Three's Company* had a pro-French Revolution agenda. Oh, and to answer your question, "Liberté, Égalité, Fraternité" is French for "Liberty, Eggs, Frat Brothers."[54]

Like music, pamphlets, newspapers, and kaleidoscopes, television shows have revolutionized the way we view the world. Were it not for the groundbreaking program, *The Cosby Show*,[55] it's possible that Barack Obama never would have become president. The landscape-changing television show, *I Love Lucy*, helped America become comfortable with

54. Trust me. I took a semester of French in college.

55. And Facebook!

the idea that women could be both self-deprecating and successful. And even *Will & Grace* paved a trailblazing path by having two leading gay characters, which eventually lead to the world's first gay Pope.

A REVOLUTIONARY FUN FACT!

Cigarette companies were allowed to sponsor revolutions up until 1971. The last revolution sponsored by a cigarette company was the Bloodied March Revolution, which ran its last commercial during *The Lawrence Welk Show*.

Yes, television has truly played an important role in changing the world. Although television isn't a "fighting revolutionary" in the sense that it doesn't directly involve mutilated political prisoners, government upheavals, and genocide in the name of a false god, television does however feature a number of programs that portray mutilated political prisoners, government upheavals, and genocide in the name of a false god. For example, *The Price Is Right*.[56]

56. And now you know why Drew Carey's hands are always covered in blood.

By learning how television has revolutionized the way we think and act, we can model our own lives to resemble those of the revolutionary fictional characters we see every Thursday at 8 p.m. on Must See TV. This is the way it's been done for centuries.

Angry about the ravages of war? "Watch *M*A*S*H!*"

Want to fight for women's right? "Watch *Murphy Brown!*"

Feeling hungry? "Eat Pringles!"[57]

The following are some of the most revolutionary shows of all time.

57. Unless you're on a diet. In which case, "Eat Cheetos!"

SHOW	TYPE	YEARS
The Ed Sullivan Show	Variety Show	1948-1971

One of the longest running variety shows on television, this pioneering show introduced America to Elvis Presley, The Beatles, and the Internet.

· ·

The Andy Griffith Show	Sitcom	1960-1968

A revolutionary show for its time, it made history for being the first show on television to portray prostitution in a positive light.

· ·

60 Minutes	Newsmagazine	1968-Present

Not only did this groundbreaking show pioneer the concept of the "newsmagazine" as we know it today, but Mike Wallace also pioneered the concept of regularly skinny-dipping with Walter Cronkite.[58]

· ·

Sesame Street	Children's Show	1968-Present

An educational children's show presented in an unprecedented way, it taught children their letters and their numbers, and taught adults that children will force adults to buy things for children.

· ·

The Mary Tyler Moore Show	Sitcom	1970-1977

One of the most revolutionary women in the past 60 years, Mary Tyler Moore was responsible for nearly overthrowing the government of France. To this day, many French citizens still fear Moore's lethal hat toss.

· ·

All in the Family	Sitcom	1971-1979

A controversial show starring the character Archie Bunker, this show taught Americans that even bigots deserve equal protection under the law.

58. So that no one else would have to.

Saturday Night Live Sketch Comedy/Variety 1975-Present

This groundbreaking comedy show forced Americans to discuss taboo subjects, as well as provide politicians with a scapegoat upon which to heap blame for society's ills. This is understandable, as the show was responsible for both the Iran hostage crisis and *Howard the Duck*.[59]

Mork & Mindy Sitcom 1978-1982

This trailblazing show starring Robin Williams and Pam Dawber, and showed viewers that aliens are just like us, only a lot more annoying.

Hill Street Blues Police Drama 1981-1987

An absolutely fearless show, *Hill Street Blues* paved the way for other revolutionary shows of their own right, including *NYPD Blue* and *The Wire*. This show is also the reason that police officers are now allowed to arrest people.

The Cosby Show Sitcom 1984-1992

Not only did this show pave the way for a larger variety of shows based on African-American culture, but it also completely redefined the sweater industry.

Live with Regis and Kathie Lee Talk Show 1988-2000

This was the first show to feature Kathie Lee Gifford, which completely revolutionized Kathie Lee Gifford.

Ellen Sitcom 1994-1998

When stand-up comedienne and actress Ellen DeGeneres came out on her similarly named TV show in 1997, she caused such a large controversy that the very gates of Hell burst open, earning her an Emmy Award.

To Catch a Predator Newsmagazine 2004-2007

In addition to proving that newsmagazines could break new ground, this show also redefined the pedophile genre.

59. Roger Ebert hated both.

A REVOLUTIONARY FUN FACT!

The bloodier the revolution, the higher the Nielsen TV Ratings. More coup d'états occur during Sweeps Week than any other time of the year.

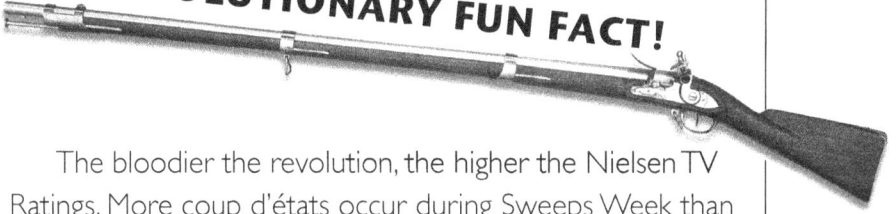

SECTION I IN REVIEW

★ Bill Gates, despite being a pescatarian, never serves fish sticks to company.

★ There are fifteen different types of revolutions, but only seven of which have been endorsed by the ADA.

★ Canada wastes everyone's time.

★ Not a single revolutionary throughout history has been lactose intolerant.

★ There are many modern revolutions raging at the moment, but ironically, only17 percent of them are solar powered.

★ Poor peasant boys are inexpensive and sold by the dozen.

★ No political pamphlet has ever been on the New York Times bestsellers list. Well, only if you don't count *The Da Vinci Code*.

★ Propaganda can be used for both good and bad. Kind of like fire. Or animal sacrifices in the name of Lucifer.

★ More protest songs were written during the Vietnam War than any other period of history, with the exception of 1985, when New Coke was introduced.

★ You know what was a good show? *Designing Women*.

Embrace the Hate: Learning to Love the Inner Revolutionary

3 attention whore? drama queen? mil!itant sex kitten bent on the wholesale destruction of social norms? (fun quiz inside!)

If life is a highway, then revolutions are the rest stop. Like regular rest stops, revolutions provide the motivation needed in order to continue on the highway of life. Like regular rest stops, revolutions are the point at which strangers can meet with a common goal and political philosophy. Like regular rest stops, revolutions provide information kiosks, vending machines, picnic areas, and gang graffiti. And a place to pee.

You've made it this far on your journey from a non-revolutionary homemaker to a yes-revolutionary warrior, but you still have quite some distance to travel.[60] In the previous chapters, you learned how revolutions have changed the past. With the knowledge you've just acquired, you can now prepare to change the future. And why stop at changing just the future? Change a tire. Change a diaper. Change a lock. Change your underwear. Change anything you would like, in any field of study. The modern revolutionary is truly a renaissance man.[61 62 63]

But wait! YOU'RE NOT A REVOLUTIONARY YET. Do you change your business cards to reflect your new occupation? Do you get that tattoo on your shoulder, the one with the skull and the evil-looking python? Are you a leftist Marxist, an anti-totalitarian libertarian, or a member of the Whig Party? Most importantly, what about your revolutionary handle-bar mustache ... is that before or after the spray-on tan?

As you can see, there are many decisions still to make. You're currently at Point A, which is to say, your boring life. You wish to arrive to Point B, also known as your revolutionary life. How do you make this transition happen? THIS CHAPTER will make this happen. Think of this chapter as Point A $\frac{1}{2}$.

In this chapter, we will answer three very important questions:
- What type of revolution do you want?
- What type of revolutionary are you?
- Against whom are you revolting?

60. Yes, I recognize that it may be difficult to believe that a revolution is like a rest stop *and* a journey. This is because revolutions can change their shape, and are also like Jell-O.

61. Starring Danny DeVito.
62. And Gregory Hines.
63. And Ed Begley, Jr.

• Have you ever been told you have your father's nose?

Do not worry. Although this may sound intimidating and quite laborious, I assure you that this section will be filled with quizzes, fun facts, and jelly.

Later in this book, we will discuss the various career opportunities, lifestyle choices, and vegan recipes available to the modern revolution. But you are not quite there yet. Before reaching this comfortable plateau of social change and government upheavals, you must first arrive at the plateau. Think of this chapter as the elevator[64] that delivers you to the plateau. Like any regular elevator, you step inside, press the button that reads, "Top Floor: Plateau," wonder if you should inform the other person in the elevator that he has terrible body odor arrive to your destination, and exit. It's a simple process, but a process nevertheless. Or as historians sometimes call it, a "process process."

So, are you ready? Are you feeling motivated? The previous chapters may have been only the revolutionary *foreplay* — but you are now about to experience the revolutionary *whatever it is that comes after foreplay!*

WHAT TYPE OF REVOLUTION DO YOU WANT?

Choosing a revolution is a lot like choosing a puppy. When you visit the pound to adopt a puppy, you don't just choose the puppy that's closest to you, pay the sad-looking woman at the cash register, and leave. Unlike a ham sandwich, a puppy isn't simple and uncomplicated, and

64. But aren't you already thinking of this chapter as Point A ½? How can you also think of this chapter as an elevator? As you will soon learn, revolutionaries — just like chapters — can be many things at once. For example, you may come across some revolutionaries who are Irish-Mexican Americans. Do not be alarmed. This is mostly perfectly normal. Do you know who hasn't put out an album in quite awhile? Pat Benatar.

nor should it be purchased as such. There are a lot of factors to take into consideration. Is the puppy smart enough to perform the Heimlich maneuver? Does the puppy have opposable thumbs? Is the puppy capable of winning the Westminster Dog Show *without* cheating, but *with* a bribe? Is the puppy aware that carbon dioxide is the No. 1 killer in the home, only after butcher knives, rolling pins, and angry spouses holding both a butcher knife and a rolling pin?

If a puppy is more complicated than a ham sandwich, then it's only natural that a revolution would be much more complicated than a puppy (the only exception of course, is if the puppy is actually eating the sandwich). Choosing a revolution is certainly not easy, as it requires planning, surveys, and a committee to choose the revolution's theme. Those who haphazardly choose a revolution without thinking through the ramifications of their decision, risk damaging their cause and essentially running an ineffective revolution.

Think I'm bluffing? Then you've clearly never heard of Denmark's "A Night Under the Sea" Revolution. Denmark chose a revolution in haste, didn't plan their theme as all the other good themes had already been chosen, and needless to say, it is unlikely that Denmark will ever again have a revolution without a theme-choosing committee. And don't get me started on their colors. All I'll say is this: those were some ugly bridesmaid/revolutionary dresses.

I cannot tell you which revolution is right for you. Choosing a revolution is an incredibly personal decision, not unlike choosing a condom. Like a condom, revolutions come in a wide variety of flavors and colors, protect from venereal diseases, and both involve Trojans. In either case, consult your doctor.

It is important that you understand that all revolutions are variations on other revolutions, which are variations of other revolutions, which are related to other revolutions, which are linked to Kevin Bacon. In this small interconnected world, both friend and foe are revolting against their enemy using ideas as old as time and methods also as old as time, but older.

In order to choose your own revolution, you must understand how they are all connected. The reason for this is simple: *backup plans*. For example, if you are fighting a violent bourgeois-democratic revolution, and you realize that it has become unsuccessful to the point that your head is no longer connected to your body,[65] you should transition to a proletarian revolt, a civil war, or even a top-down seizure of power. It's also suggested that you visit a hospital.[66]

The following graphic explains the Family Tree of Revolutions. Naturally, the name is derived from the shape of a tree, as well as the Family Revolution of 1983, in which Dad told Justin to stop hitting Cherie or he was going to turn this car around.

65. Hope you have a good HMO!

66. Unless you're busy and have stuff to do.

The Family Tree of Revolutions

UNEMPLOYMENT REVOLUTION

SEXUAL REVOLUTION

KILLER ROBOT REVOLUTION

Bored?

PEACEFUL REVOLUTION

Nice Robots?

Boycotting...

Mean Robots?

WOMEN'S RIGHTS REVOLUTION

Sorry, We're All Out.

PROLETARIAT REVOLUTION

Picketing...

Doesn't "Top-Down" Sound Kinky?

GAY RIGHTS REVOLUTION

Now!

Bottom-Up Revolt

Top-Down Revolt

Two Women at Once?

Robots?

Striking...

With Women

Culture, Music & Fashion!

When Do We Want It?

An Evil Corporation!

The Government!

Inequality!

Science & Technology!

Wasn't *Jaws IV: The Revenge* a great movie?

Fight Against...

CIVIL RIGHTS REVOLUTION

Peace!

Yes

VIOLENT REVOLUTIONS

Centaur

Social Change

What Do We Want?

No

NON-VIOLENT REVOLUTIONS

Are You a Shark?

Are You a Violent Animal?

Yes

No

AGRICULTURAL REVOLUTION

ANIMAL REVOLUTION

MINERAL REVOLUTION

Vegetable!

Animal!

Mineral!

YOUR REVOLUTION IS...

WHAT TYPE OF REVOLUTIONARY ARE YOU?

You've chosen your revolution and you have your outfit picked out. But what kind of revolutionary are you actually going to be? Many people are often surprised to learn that there is more than one type of revolutionary; although to be fair, some people are also surprised to learn that the world isn't actually round.[67]

67. Anymore.

As a popular T-shirt maker once said, "Lead, follow, or get out of the way." Now sure, some may incorrectly attribute this quote to Thomas Paine. As we've learned by now, Mr. Paine was quite sarcastic, which is why this quote is actually attributed to Big Dogs Apparel. But what exactly does this mean — to lead, follow, or get out of the way — and how does this apply? Are we allowed to "follow" behind a mini-van with a "Baby On Board" sign in traffic? What if an elderly person on a Rascal mobility scooter is chasing you — is this considered "leading?" Do you still have to "get out of the way" of a speeding train if you find a quarter on the tracks? What if it's a quarter, a dime, and two nickels?[68]

68. Nope.

Now you understand the moral dilemma. If you do

not posses the answers to these questions, how will you determine your place in a revolution? Are you leading a revolution? Are you following a revolution? Where are the restrooms located in a revolution? If a train leaves Cincinnati at 3:30 and a train leaves Baltimore at 4:45, in what city are the train's passengers most likely to overthrow the government?

As anyone who's ever watched a professional sports team, a marching band, or the television show *Captain Planet* will attest, everyone in a team has a role. Some teams have a drum major, who is responsible for leading the other instruments. Some teams have a quarterback, who is responsible for backing quarters. Some teams even have a whiny little kid, who is responsible for being picked on. Structure and roles are important in sports, jobs, bands, governments, and jewel heists, so it's only natural that revolutions would be the same.

Like joining the Masons or living in communist China, you can't just sign up.[69] Not only is deciding one's own role in a revolution unethical, but it also removes all the mystery and the fun. You must discover your role organically. For that reason, I've included the following important quiz. Although the questions in the quiz appear to be somewhat random, each question has been *carefully* chosen, as they each reveal a unique trait about your psyche.

69. Anymore.

Answer these questions as honestly as you can, take the finished quiz to a bank to be notarized, and then revel in the knowledge that you now have a role in your revolution.

Remember: No cheating. God and/or Santa is/are watching.

QUIZ:
WHAT ROLE DO YOU PLAY IN A REVOLUTION?

★★★★★★★★★★★★★

1. If you were making a pie out of fruit, and you also happened to be a fruit yourself, you would be:

    a) An orange

    b) A papaya

    c) A banana

    d) A mango

    e) A date

    f) Some weird papaya/apple hybrid

2. You're walking down the street and you run into an old friend from high school. This isn't just any old friend, but the bully who used to torment you. You also used to think his mom was hot. Do you:

    a) Ignore him and walk the other way.

    b) Ask him for the time and, while he looks at his watch, shank him in the shoulder and run.

    c) When he recognizes you and waves, pretend that you don't speak English. Or French.

    d) Give him a few spare dollars, because he's homeless. But if he's homeless, why is he wearing that fur coat?

    e) Subtly ask him if his mother is still around. Spray him with mace when he takes offense.

    f) Become his gay lover. Kind of ironic that you used to think that his mother was hot, right?

3. Speaking of hardware, you feel most at home when you're using:

    a) A chainsaw

    b) A pair of pliers

    c) A hammer

    d) A chainsaw without the chain, also known as a saw

    e) A level

    f) A screwdriver, hold the ice

4. Your beliefs towards imbibing alcohol are as follows:

    a) Drinking should be illegal.

    b) There's nothing wrong with a drink now and again.

    c) Drinking should be made illegal, made legal again, and then remade even more super illegal.

    d) Where am I? Whose clothes are these? How did I get here?

    e) No seriously, how did I get here? And who are you? Why am I in this sling?

    f) Drinking should still be illegal.

5. The whole is greater than the sum of its:

    a) Hearts

    b) Carts

    c) Darts

    d) Tarts

    e) Charts

    f) Pieces

6. If you had to sacrifice just one personal living thing, it would be:

    a) Your Labrador retriever

    b) Your first-born son

    c) Your wife

    d) Your mother-in-law

    e) Your wife's mother

    f) The woman who gave birth to your wife

7. When it comes to religion, you believe that:

    a) There is a god somewhere out there, but he doesn't play a significant part in your life.

    b) Jesus saves, over $30 off the retail price, this Labor Day weekend.

    c) "Religion is the opiate of the masses," a defense which has never held up in a drug conviction.

    d) A church that gives out free coffee and donuts is the church for you.

    e) There can't possibly be a god, because he wouldn't let bad things like floods, genocide, and Canadians happen.

    f) The only insurance you need is Jesus. And that, officer, is why I don't have proof of insurance.

8. If a tree falls in a forest, it:

    a) Does make a sound.

    b) Does not make a sound.

    c) Doesn't make a sound unless it falls on a mime.

    d) Screams like a little girl.

    e) Breaks its pelvis, and spends its twilight years in a nursing home

    f) Lands on its feet, like a cat, but without the tail.

9. Sex should:

    a) Be conducted between a man and a woman.

    b) Only occur between two consenting adults.

    c) Take place through a hole in a sheet.

    d) Be necessary for the creation of children. And to punish adults.

    e.) Happen online.

    f.) Not happen tonight dear, because I have a headache.

10. Your life's philosophy can be best described as follows:

    a) "Whate'er thou art, act well thy part."

    b) "Political power grows out of the barrel of a gun."

c) "He who denied it, supplied it."

d) "Silence is argument carried out by other means."

e) "On the roller coaster of life, there are ups, there are downs, and sometimes people throw up on you."

f) "Life is life a box of chocolates. If you leave it in the car in the sun for too long, it will melt."

Now that you've finished the quiz, count your answers to see if any one letter comes up more than the others.

The following key will help you determine your role in the revolution.

KEY TO THE QUIZ

★★★★★★★★★★★★★

If you answered a) more than any other answer: You are THE LEADER
The Leader is the central figure in any revolution. Like Che Guevara or Col. Sanders, it is The Leader who leads the troops into battles, sounds the rally cry, and gets to wear the big hat, which reads, "I'm the Boss." If it were not for The Leader, the entire revolution would shrivel up on the vine and die. This is of course, assuming the revolution is a tomato. It is worth pointing out that the only thing more important in a revolution than The Leader is the rifle. The second thing more important than The Leader is a decent healthcare plan.

If you answered b) more than any other answer: You are THE BRAINS

Somebody has to determine the best strategy, figure out the difficult multiplication tables, and write all that tricky HTML code for the revolution. This person, of course, is The Brains. The smartest member of any revolution, The Brains is known for his bright intellect and his nerdy-looking glasses. Nobody makes fun of him however, because only he knows the square root of blowing you up.

If you answered c) more than any other answer: You are THE MUSCLE

If your revolution is going to turn violent, then you will need The Muscle. Just as a submarine cannot exist without someone cheekily asking if it's "filled with seamen,"[70] a revolution cannot exist without The Muscle's brawn and power. The Muscle comes in a wide variety of shapes and sizes — such as assassin, storm trooper, and dumb jock — and thus is the cornerstone of a revolution. This is because from a distance, he actually looks like a cornerstone.[71]

70. This reminds me of a joke. Question: What's long, hard, and employed for military nautical missions? Answer: A penis! Get it?

71. He's also made out of cement.

If you answered d) more than any other answer: You are THE FINANCIER

What, do you think revolutions are free? If that was the case, they would be given away on crackers by old women in hairnets at Costco. Revolutions cost money — a lot of money — and this is why The Financier is essential. Contrary to popular belief, The Financier is not always Jewish. He is however, usually thin and agitated. In the past, The Financier used to come from old money on the Upper East Side of New York; now he hails from a Web-based company that's only been around for six months, before being sold for several billion dollars. He's also the one who signs your paycheck.

If you answered e) more than any other answer: You are THE FOREIGNER

Have you ever tried making General Tso's chicken without a Mexican person helping in the kitchen? Impossible, right? A revolution without at least one foreign influence is no different. Often overlooked but never under-appreciated, The Foreigner plays an essential role in the revolution. Even a small neighborhood that wishes to do battle with an imperialistic landlord must employ at least one outside source. It is important to note that the ethnicity and race of The Foreigner may be of any origin except Dutch. No one knows why this is.[72]

72. Except for the Italians.

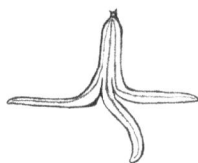

If you answered f) more than any other answer: You are THE WITTY MASCOT

Where would the world be if it were not for the comic relief? Most sociologists agree that the world would probably be in a better place. Nevertheless, The Witty Mascot is the yin to the average revolutionary's yang, and provides the necessary quick zings and witty comebacks needed to bring about social change. Some of the more well-known Witty Mascot revolutionaries include Abbie Hoffman and Hristo Botev, the latter of whom was known for his hilarious prop comedy.

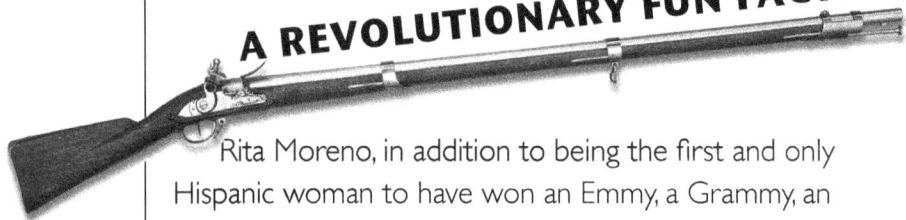

> ## A REVOLUTIONARY FUN FACT!
>
> Rita Moreno, in addition to being the first and only Hispanic woman to have won an Emmy, a Grammy, an Oscar, and a Tony, is one of only two women to have fought back the German army with a curling iron and a saber.
> This feat later won her yet another Oscar.

WHO ARE YOU REVOLTING AGAINST?

You're mad as hell and you're not going to take it anymore. But against whom are you going to take it out? Your mail carrier, who's faithfully delivered your mail for the past thirty years, through rain, sleet, and snow? Of course not, he has a daughter in college.[73] What about that Uruguayan rugby team who crashed in the Andes Mountains in 1972 and resorted to cannibalism? Don't blame them for your frustration; you too would eat a human being if you were stranded and hungry.[74]

As a revolutionary, you need to learn to channel your rage, and instead take it out on those who actually deserve such assaults: for example, the government, big business, or

73. And you don't want him to start opening your mail again.

74. For crying out loud, you eat at McDonald's, so you're clearly not that picky when it comes to food.

every single political idea that isn't your own. Just because you happen to have the revolutionary tools in your revolutionary toolbox that you bought from a revolutionary hardware store, doesn't give you the right to use your revolutionary tools on every Tom, Dick, and Harriet.[75] In fact, determining a target upon which to inflict your revolutionary anger is one of the most important decisions you can make, only after choosing a font.[76]

Why is knowing who you're revolting against so important? Turkish president and revolutionary Mustafa Kemal Ataturk said it best when he said: "I specifically asked that this Reuben sandwich not have Thousand Island dressing. Who's responsible for this?" Translated into English, this means: "Always know your enemy."

Choosing a target can be difficult, and, for this reason, a number of methods have sprung up over the years, to aid in making this difficult decision. Some of the more popular methods include playing darts, a round of backgammon, and a stirring session of charades; however, no single method is preferable when it comes to choosing a revolution's target. You may choose any of the aforementioned methods, or come up with one on your own, except for karaoke.[77] I've even heard of some rabble-rousers who decide to revolt against an authoritative corporation, simply because the corporation was located only a block from the tavern, and everyone was too drunk to walk any further. Another popular way of choosing a target is to flip a coin, provided it's a two-sided coin.

75. Harry, in drag.

76. Might I suggest Helvetica?

77. Unless it's "Don't Stop Believing" by Journey.

Regardless of how you choose your target, what does matter is that you do so in a timely manner. It is important that you not delay your anger. The following is a pie chart of the most popular targets, as well as their descriptions. While I hesitate to suggest one target over another, I do however encourage you to study each of the following and become angry at the target that best suits your needs.

? A REVOLUTIONARY QUIZ ?

You consider the corporation Wal-Mart to be:

A) An evil, hedonistic company.

B) A patriarchal institution, existing solely for the suppression of women.

C) A greedy business whose largest priority is profits over civil rights.

D) A great place to buy diapers and discount jars of mustard.

POPULAR TARGETS IN RECENT REVOLUTIONS

Government

The government has long been a popular target throughout history, as it can be blamed for everything from voter suppression to prison riots. Have a cold? Hate the attorney general? Tired of the increasing price of stamps? Angry

Revolutionary Targets

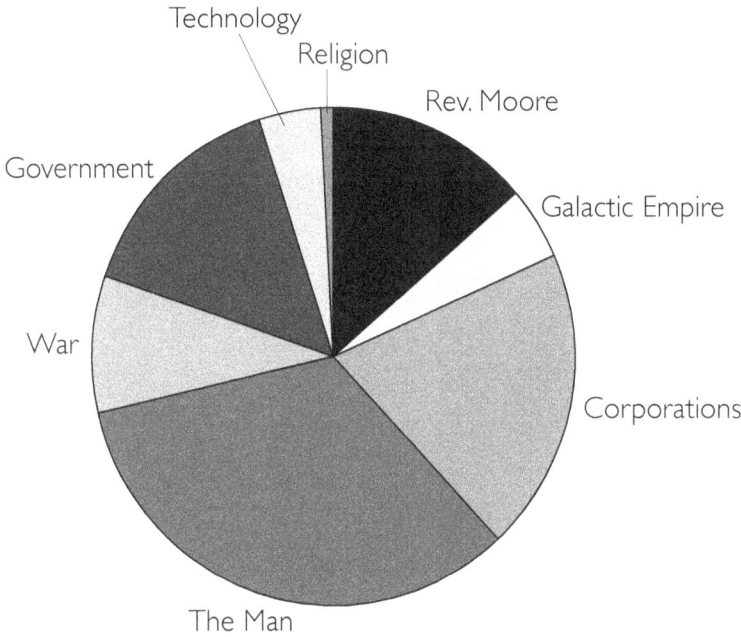

because there isn't a Truman Capote national holiday? Fed up with broccoli soup? Think your third grade teacher's puffy cheeks made her look like a chipmunk? Disappointed that the president has never appointed an anarchist as the Secretary of State?[78] Annoyed that Dane Cook still has a career despite the fact that unemployment exists in the world? All this — and more — can be blamed on the government. Make the government your target.

78. If you don't count Warren Christopher.

Corporations

Nobody likes their job. Even those who lie and say they like their job are usually lying. Nevertheless, we all find ways to survive our jobs by taking coffee breaks, lunch breaks, smoke breaks, and lobster bisque breaks. However, any time a corporation threatens to lower wages or introduce rats back into the factory, it can be expected that they will soon have a revolution on their hands. Corporations understand that they cannot exist without their workers, but what they don't realize is that their workers cannot exist without oxygen. Therefore, anytime a corporation takes away its employees' dignity, holiday pay, or lobster bisque breaks,[79] they can expect to become the target of a revolution.

79. As was the case in *Norma Rae*.

War

All may be fair in love and war, but the difference between the two is that in war, you can't get a restraining order. While most normal revolutionaries understand that only blood and bad attitudes will effect the change needed in this world, the anti-war revolutionary, or "peace activist," believes that violence under any circumstance is unnecessary. Some of the better-known peace activists include Khan Abdul Ghaffar Khan, Bishop Oscar Romero, and Yoko Ono. Unfortunately, most peace activists only find success after marrying a member of The Beatles, as was the case with Khan Abdul Ghaffar Khan, Bishop Oscar Romero, and Yoko Ono.

The Man

It isn't entirely clear who or what "The Man" is. All you know is that you need to stick it to him. This doesn't necessarily mean that The Man is any less dangerous or worthy of being targeted in a revolution. Terms such as "business casual," "the war on drugs,"" and "stay off my lawn, you damn kids," are just some of the victims of The Man. While The Man is more loosely defined than some of the other targets of revolutionaries, The Man is nonetheless prone to attacks from hippies, stoners, rebels, and emo kids who listen to indie music.

Religion

Some people rollerblade. Some people watch birds. And some people think the idea of organized religion is a corrupt manipulation of the malleable human mind. Religion has long been under attack throughout history, by people ranging from atheists and communists, to rollerblading birdwatchers.[80] Revolutions have also benefited religion as well. A revolt against the Catholic Church brought about Lutheranism in 1517, and a later revolt against the Lutheran Church brought about Lutheranism 2: The Saga Continues in 1742. If you doubt the presence of God, Allah, Jehovah, or whatever it is that Scientologists believe in,[81] then you may be interested in targeting religion in your revolution.

80. In other words, communists.

81. Tom Cruise.

Technology

It's not worth explaining how to revolt against technology, because odds are you're not a Luddite if you're reading this book on a Kindle.[82]

82. By candlelight.

Galactic Empire

Sometimes the target of your revolution is clearly defined. There's no question who you're revolting against if you're a woman (an oppressive patriarchal society), or you despise the government (all politicians), or you're gay (homophobia), or a Chihuahua (anything taller than three inches). But what if you're a mutant, an alien, or a weird robot thing? Naturally, you'll want to rebel against the Galactic Empire. While technically anyone can fight against the Galactic Empire — whether Jedi or non-Jedi — it's generally advised that you at least join the Rebel Alliance, as they're the only ones with a decent health care plan.

The Reverend from *Footloose*

Of all the adversaries, targets, and enemies throughout history, there are two which have angered revolutionaries more than anything else: the government, and Reverend Shaw Moore from the film *Footloose*. Also known as the evil reverend who just wouldn't let the kids dance, Reverend Shaw Moore inspired not just Kevin Bacon, but literally generations of revolutionaries to rise in a fierce united rage, as well as kicking off their Sunday shoes.

A REVOLUTIONARY FUN FACT!

In the future, revolutions will be fought by robots. And not the nice ones.

4 becoming a nonconforming, independent, anarchist revolutionary: the rules and regulations

When a person becomes the President of the United States, that person is sworn in under the oath of office. In doing so, the President promises to uphold the constitution, protect the American people, and to take a breathalyzer test[83] before making calls to foreign leaders. The position of President of the United States is an important and serious one, and thus any jokes or snickers should be kept to a minimum. Unlike a circus ringmaster or a USDA food safety inspector, the responsibilities for President are clearly laid out and defined.

A revolutionary, however, is the antithesis of a U.S.

83. Or a urine test, as was the case with George W. Bush.

President; revolutionaries have no rules outlining their responsibilities, right? WRONG. Although it's possible that a revolutionary will find himself fighting against this very same president,[84] parallels nevertheless exist between the two. Like the President, the revolutionary must agree to keep certain promises and oaths. Failure to do so will result in punishment and, in a few rare cases, death. On the bright side, not all oath-breaking revolutionaries are put to death, as opposed to 78 percent of all U.S. Presidents.

This strict adherence to moral codes and conducts brings an unwanted challenge to the modern revolutionary's life. On the one hand, you strongly desire to change the world through new and challenging ways; on the other hand, you are required to follow a code of conduct or face being ostracized by the revolutionary community. How are you to resolve this moral dilemma? Or worse, with both hands filled with hypothetical situations, how will you to clap at the opera?[85]

The pain of the moral dilemma you will face as a revolutionary is similar to walking around everyday with a pebble in your shoe. Painful, right? Now imagine that instead of a pebble, you had a six inch piece of barbed wire fencing. Not only would you wish you had a pebble instead of the piece of barbed wire fencing, but it would undoubtedly put you into such a dour mood that would you find little joy in life. This is not unlike the agony a revolutionary feels on a daily basis.[86]

Being a revolutionary means living by an ethical code of conduct. Those who ignore such covenants are in peril

84. The one making drunken phone calls to foreign leaders.

85. Hire the poor peasant boy from Chapter 2.

86. Although if you had just taken the barbed wire out of your shoe, we wouldn't be experiencing this terrible metaphor in the first place.

of having their revolutionary privileges revoked. Further, some are even punished by having to wear those awful barbed wire shoes.

Do you believe you have what it takes to be a revolutionary? If so, you must be willing to live by The Revolutionary Code of Conduct.

IN THEIR OWN REVOLUTIONARY WORDS

"If you tremble with indignation at every injustice, then you are a comrade of mine. If you're still trembling after fighting injustice, then you may just want to put on a sweater."

CHE GUEVARA
Marxist Revolutionary

THE REVOLUTIONARY CODE OF CONDUCT

1. I AM A REVOLUTIONARY, and thus pledge to only overthrow those governments that are immoral, including those who practice secret murders, embezzle from its citizens, or engage in blatant nepotism, with the exception of those government employees that happen to be related to me.

2. I AM A REVOLUTIONARY, and thus pledge to only denounce those corporations that are huge and evil global conglomerates. This is especially true if the corporation's CEO smokes a cigar while checking the pocket watch he keeps in his vest pocket, and guffaws menacingly.[87]

3. I AM A REVOLUTIONARY, and thus will refrain from punching orphans, stealing candy from babies, and punching candy that's shaped to look like orphans.

4. I AM A REVOLUTIONARY, and thus agree to make my credit card payments on time — unless I am prevented from doing so, due to the existence

87. Oh, and strokes a white cat.

of injustice in the world. If this is the case, and injustice continues to exist, then I will be forgiven of any and all credit card debt.

5. I AM A REVOLUTIONARY, and thus pledge to promote social change, equitable access to justice, and impartial but effective politics in 30 minutes or less... or your money back.

6. I AM A REVOLUTIONARY, and thus promise to have a level head at all times and in all places. Exceptions may apply if I am in battle, overthrowing a head of state, or if I've had a few beers in a tavern and somebody says something with which I disagree.

7. I AM A REVOLUTIONARY, and thus will be courteous at all times, such as helping an old lady cross the street. If it is discovered that the aforementioned old lady is a communist and I happen to be a fiercely devout anti-communist American, then pushing her in front of oncoming traffic will not only be encouraged, but rewarded.[88]

8. I AM A REVOLUTIONARY, and thus agree to share my possessions with others in a spirit of common ownership and brotherhood. If it is discovered that I am not sharing 100 percent of my possessions, then I will be punished by being forced to share my possessions with others in a spirit of common ownership and brotherhood.

9. I AM A REVOLUTIONARY, and thus will not take up arms against those who are my friends, my neighbors, avowed pacifists, the elderly,[89] religious leaders, or anyone who owes me money, as it's difficult to collect money from a dead person.

10. I AM A REVOLUTIONARY, and thus will dedicate my life to forcing those around me to agree with my worldview. Or I will just change my own worldview. Whichever is easier.

Please sign this code of contact, have your two witnesses sign it, have them state their blood type, and note the moon's position in the sky.

Thank you.

88. Probably with a coffee mug with your face on it, or a glow-in-the-dark keychain.

89. Unless the elderly person is a communist; see No. 7.

_____   _____
Name   Date

_____   _____   _____   _____
Witness 1   Blood Type   Witness 2   Blood Type

_____
Moon's Position in the Sky (in degrees)

A WARNING ABOUT "COMMUNISM"

One mistake that many inexperienced revolutionaries make early in their revolutionary career, is diving into communism too quickly. As many are surprised to learn, being a communist is not *technically* required to be a revolutionary. In fact, many inexperienced revolutionaries are also surprised to learn that some people — known as "capitalists" and "communist haters" — do not approve of such a lifestyle at all.

It is possible to emulate Karl Marx without going full throttle and diving completely into communism; for example, dressing up as Santa Claus and charging children a fair market price for their gifts. Sure, it's tempting to want a classless society — but that does not necessarily mean it's classy. These are not the same thing. In fact, if you were to go to a party hosted by the Young Capitalists of America and announce in a loud voice, "I'm a commie-loving Marxist! Anyone want to do Jell-O shots?" it's likely that you would be looked down upon. Again, this is not classy.

There is certainly a time and place for communism, such as Cuba, or 3:30 p.m. But that does not mean that it is for everyone, or that it is even for you. If you find yourself considering the communism lifestyle, be sure to ask yourself the following questions:

1.) Do I have a problem with common ownership?
2.) Am I Ronald Reagan?

If you answered "yes" to any of these questions, then communism may not be right for you.

FORMING A BELIEF SYSTEM FOR YOUR REVOLUTION

What do you believe? You probably don't know what you believe. In fact, studies have shown that 84 percent of Americans are more likely to believe a completely fabricated study than they are to know what they believe. If you don't know what you believe, can you still be an effective revolutionary? Not only will you be ineffective, but odds are that you'll move on to other pastimes, like raping and pillaging, or knitting a sweater. A revolutionary who doesn't know what he believes in is similar to a ship without a rudder, or a hull, or a bow, or a crew. Unless it's a ghost crew. In which case —— yikes!

Knowing what you believe in is the most integral part of what makes you, you. It's more important than your heart, or your savings account, or your adopted children.[90] Understanding what you believe in will provide you with a moral compass in life. Not sure whether to steal that stranger's wallet? Unsure whether you should stab your adversary in the neck? What about lying to prison officials, is that allowed or condemned? Simply look at your moral compass and your answer will appear: "south/east." Problem solved.[91]

You've chosen the revolution to which you will belong, and so now is the time to choose the most important aspect of all: constructing your belief system. While ideals — much like a fungus or religious superstitions[92] — grow over

90. C'mon, they're only adopted. They're not your tchildren.

91. If you are facing north, it is unlikely that your moral compass will read "south/east."

92. And interest, compounded daily.

time, you will first want to determine the base upon which to place your beliefs. Only after doing this, will your life's philosophy grow organically, not unlike a factory.

The following is a step-by-step process that will direct you in constructing your revolution's mission statement. Be sure not to skip any steps, for doing so may result in paralysis, or worse, confusion.

CONSTRUCTING YOUR REVOLUTION'S MISSION STATEMENT

1. All Mission Statements Must Begin With "I"

It is imperative that all mission statements begin with "I." The primary reason for this is so there is no confusion as to whom the mission statement is being directed.[93] Mission statements that begin with "you" or "them" or "we the people" are amateur at best, as nothing good has ever come from them. A mission statement which begins with "eye" is also acceptable.

2. Reference the Year You Became a Revolutionary

Any company worth its salt will reference the year it was established in its mission statement. If you too wish to be worth salt, you will need to do the same. If you are unsure which year it is, do not hesitate to consult a wristwatch, a sundial, or a pair of dice for verification. While estimating within ten years in either direction is allowed, it is best that you check with your local congressman.

93. This one time, a complete stranger on the subway began to write a mission statement for me and he was homeless and reeked of alcohol and it was hilarious and, well, you had to be there.

3. The Mission Statement Must Be Derived from an Established Philosophy

A mission statement cannot simply be a collection of good intentions and hopeful desires. If this were the case, all you would need to do is plagiarize any random child's letter from the offices of the Make-a-Wish Foundation. In order to find a life philosophy that best suits your revolutionary ambitions, be sure to graduate from a college that is renowned for its philosophy department; for example, the Danville Community Technical School of Air Conditioning Maintenance.

4. You Must Define Yourself In Your Mission Statement

This is the place for you to shine. Here you will define your role in the revolution you've chosen for yourself; your view of the government; your marital status, your horoscope sign, your sexual orientation, your current religion, your race and ethnicity, your opinion of progressive folk-rock band Jethro Tull, and whether you believe peanut butter on celery is a bastardized way of eating one's vegetables. It is absolutely vital that this section be as personal as possible, as revolutionary critics can smell impersonalization a mile away. To be fair, many revolutionary critics are a hybrid of part human, part hunting dog.

5. The Mission Statement Must Be Short

94. And so are children, apparently.

Life is short.[94] Therefore, a mission statement that continues past two pages is likely to be ignored by the world at large. Although the mission of a mission statement isn't necessarily to draw attention to the revolutionary, it nevertheless has to be marketable in the rare case that it ends up being plastered on a mug or a T-shirt.[95] You never know when a phrase from your mission statement — whether it be "viva la revolution" or "where do babies come from" will become commercially viable in the future.

IN THEIR OWN REVOLUTIONARY WORDS

"O God! That one might read the book of fate, and see the revolution of the times make mountains level, and might Henry Wriothesley, 3rd Earl of Southampton strip down so that his bosom may be visible, and ... Oh sorry, was I being gay again?"

WILLIAM SHAKESPEARE
English Playwright and Poet

INFORMING YOUR FRIENDS AND FAMILY ABOUT YOUR NEW LIFESTYLE

Becoming a revolutionary is unquestionably the most important event that can occur in your life. "But aren't there other life events that are more important?" Of course not. If that were the case, this book would be titled, "Falling in Love for Fun and Profit" or perhaps "Hosting a Bar Mitzvah on $30 a Day for Fun and Profit." But it's not. It's about revolutions. Hence, revolutions are the most important event that can occur in your life.

Becoming a revolutionary is more important than:

- Your high school graduation
- Your college graduation
- Meeting your college girlfriend
- Your wedding
- The birth of your child
- Landing that new job
- Your affair with the crazy hot secretary, the one whose breasts are the size of China, and whose legs go all the way up to Beijing
- Your divorce
- Your second wedding

Becoming a revolutionary is not only the most important thing you'll ever do, but it is also the most consistent. Like fashion or breakfast pastries, revolutions do not change. The revolution you were fighting 150 years ago will still be the same revolution you are fighting today. Plus, you're in a wheelchair. Don't feel bad — most people over the age of 150 are in wheelchairs.[96]

96. Speaking of old people in wheelchairs, did you know that Franklin D. Roosevelt is still alive in a nursing home somewhere? It's true! Warren G. Harding told me.

Like any important event in your life, you will want to share this momentous occasion with everyone you know. And what does this usually entail? Receptions! Invitations! Gowns! Cocktail sausages! Dry cleaning bills, because somebody thought it would be a bright idea to eat cocktail sausages while wearing a gown! Yes, announcing your new-found calling in life as a revolutionary is truly an event to be remembered and shared. Sometimes both.

But what if you don't have the money to throw a revolutionary reception? As it turns out, the reception is not technically necessary. For example, what if the only gay men who ever came out of the closet were the gay millionaires who could afford to pay for the coming out parties? Happily, that is not the world we live in, since coming out of the closet as a gay man requires little more than a gossipy friend, a cocktail napkin, and a Sharpie.

Fortunately for you and other cash-strapped revolutionary wannabes, the reception is not important, as much as is the announcement. If you are coming out as a revolutionary, a simple paper declaration distributed to your friends, family, co-workers, and political enemies will suffice. For those of you who happen to be Martin Luther, be sure to nail a copy of your declaration to the door of a very large building, such as a church, school auditorium, or local Wal-Mart. The following is an example of such a declaration, which you may copy and distribute at your own leisure.

Don't skimp on the envelope. It makes you look cheap. Also, use scented stationary if available.[97]

97. It's *always* available.

DEAR FRIENDS, FAMILY, CO-WORKERS AND POLITICAL ENEMIES:

This is to inform you that _____(your name)_____ *is now a* _____(type of revolutionary)_____ *revolutionary, in the cause of the* _____(type of revolution)_____ *revolution.*

As you know, _____(your name)_____ *has been quite* (happy/ unhappy/overcome with food sickness) *with the local* (big business/ government/quality of hot dogs at the corner 7-11) *in which he is currently* (employed/governed/employed) *. This is primarily due to the fact that* (his company is shipping his job to China/the government is systematically murdering people/his 7-11 hot dog is made from murdered Chinese people) *.*

Now as _____(your name)'s_____ *closest* _____(friend/family/political enemy)_____ *, you will understandably be alarmed. There are no doubt many questions running through your mind, such as:*

- *What lifestyle choices will this change entail for* __(your name)__ *?*
- *Do I have to treat* _____(your name)_____ *differently?*
- *As a revolutionary, will* _____(your name)_____ *still be allowed to* _____(go to church/have sex/impersonate Ethel Merman in that seedy cabaret that was shut down for serving alcohol to minors while simultaneously running an illegal pyramid scheme)_____ *?*

The short answer to these questions is "no." The long answer to these questions is "certainly and definitely no."

Despite your concerns and misgivings, you should rest assured that _____(your name)_____ *is becoming a revolutionary out of the goodness of* _____(your name)'s_____ _____(heart/soul/the song that Tom Hanks played on the giant keyboard in the movie Big)_____ *. You* __(did/did not)__ *do anything wrong. As it turns out,* _____(your name)_____ *has felt this way for a* __(very)__ *long time, and nothing you* _____(could/could not)_____ *have done would have made any difference. Rest assured that this* (is/is not/is totally)_____ *your fault.*

You can support _____(your name)_____ *in* _____(his/her/a man in women's clothing/RuPaul's)_____ *new decision by reading the accompanied literature, "What to Do When a Loved One Becomes a Revolutionary." You can also support* _____(your name)_____ *by not mentioning* (big business/the government/salmonella poisoning) *around* (him/her)_____ , *or by* _____(having that mole on your face removed, because let's be honest, everyone's talking).

Lastly, it is important to remember that _____(your name)_____ *is still the same person you've always known* _____(and loved)_____ . *With the small exception that* _____(your name)_____ *no longer takes showers.*

I hope you don't mind that _____(your name)_____ *wrote this declaration in the 3rd person. It may feel awkward, but you'll have to get used to it. That's what revolutionaries do.*

Revolutionary Yours,

____(your name, but spelled correctly this time)____

P.S. By the way, _____(your name)_____ *has registered his revolution at* ____(Williams & Sonoma/Target/Bed, Bath & Beyond)____ .

? A REVOLUTIONARY QUIZ ?

You assume the U.S. Government will:

A) Initiate unnecessary wars against third-world
   countries, in a fruitless attempt at securing more
   oil.

B) Tread on your civil rights by eavesdropping on
   your conversation and opening your mail.

C) Take away your right to marry your life-partner
   in a fascist attempt to promote supposed family
   values.

D) Mail your welfare check by Tuesday.

SECTION II IN REVIEW

★ Members of the Whig Party are called Whiggies — on purpose.

★ A puppy is more complicated than a ham sandwich.

★ There are three types of revolutions: vegetable, animal, and mineral.

★ Quizzes are always both fun and educational, but only sometimes lethal.

★ Every enemy of a revolutionary is chosen from a pie chart.

★ Revolutionaries don't smile, but they do have a 6" piece of barbed wire in their shoe.

★ Stay clear of communism. Unless you're a communist. Then it's OK.

★ There are five steps to creating a revolutionary mission statement. There's also a bonus step — an "Easter egg" — hidden somewhere in the DVD menu.

★ Your wife knows about your affair with your secretary. She's not stupid. But she is Canadian.

★ Soda water will get a cocktail sausage stain out of a gown (unverified).

The Brass Tacks of a Revolution: Because Somebody Broke the Stapler

5 grease is the word: but there are still others to choose from

You know what's a funny word to say? Kiwi. Nobody named "Kiwi" is ever taken seriously. You know what's an even funnier word to say? "Schziotrefalgarunbuz." No matter how you say it, it's going to sound as if you're having a stroke while smoking peyote. Plus, you'll be accused of making up words that don't exist.

Language is made up of words, words are made up of letters, and if you look closely you'll also see that letters are made up of germs, which is why you should always wear gloves when handling the alphabet. Different words connote different feelings and emotions, and so as a revolutionary, you must always be conscious of the words you use in your everyday conversations. To say, "I want to SHAKE your hand," is to imply you come in peace. To say, "I want to LIQUIFY your hand," is to imply that you come in violence and war. Or, you're a blender.

Employing the correct words is especially important when it comes to choosing a name for your revolution. You may think that when it comes to your revolution, believing in a life-changing philosophy or having enough dinnerware are your top priorities. This is not so. If you accomplish just one goal today, let it be finding a suitable name for your revolution. Finding an appropriate name is similar to remembering to turn the oven off before you leave your house — to forget such a simple but important task is to accept the fact that your house will burn down.

Why is naming a revolution so important? A name is the first thing others will see when encountering your revolution. It is the first thing your enemies will read when you hand them your business card.[98] Having the right or wrong name can make or break your revolution, as the right name will instill fear into the hearts of all those who hear it, while the wrong name will provoke fits of laughter until those who hear it inevitably end up tearing their hair out, leading to baldness.[99]

Is having the correct name really *that* important? Consider the following true example, which will prove how important a correct and appropriate name is. You've

98. But don't hand your business card to your enemies *too* quickly, or you'll give them a papercut!

99. And death.

no doubt heard of the "Russian Revolution" — but did you know that it actually took place in Cleveland, Ohio? General Guillermo H. Wescott, while leading his brigade on a revolt against the United States over transgender labor laws in 1917, accidentally assigned the task of naming the revolution to his unemployed brother-in-law, a man named Russian Smith. Naturally, Russian Smith chose to name the revolution after himself, which is how it received the name of the "Russian Revolution." To combat the eventual confusion that this caused, Gen. Wescott later founded the country of Greenland, which he named due to it's abundance of greenery and vegetation.[100]

100. Which, strangely, looks like ice.

As you can see, naming your revolution is very important, even more so than doing your taxes, or remembering history correctly. Should you choose an appropriate name, and come up with a catchy revolutionary slogan, you may possibly go down in history as one of the greatest revolutionaries in history. This chapter will show you how.

IN THEIR OWN REVOLUTIONARY WORDS

"It is not the name of your revolution that is important, but rather the word by which everybody calls your revolution. In other words, it is the name that is important. Also, mojitos are important. I'm an alcoholic."

ERNEST HEMINGWAY
U.S. Author and Nobel Prize Winner

WHAT WILL YOU CALL YOUR REVOLUTION?

Imagine that your parents named you Shirley when you were born, despite the fact that you are male. You would most likely be made fun of while growing up in elementary school. Students would taunt you, chanting "Shirley, Shirley, that's a name for girls! All you're missing are your earrings and pearls!" Kids can be very cruel sometimes, over something as simple and benign as a name. I know this, because this once happened to a woman I once knew. She later changed her name to Kevin.[101]

Regardless of whether you're naming a person or naming a revolution, names will always be very important. In fact, the baby-naming book industry is worth well over $18 billion dollars, proving that any parent who names their newborn "John" or "Emily" probably doesn't know how to read.[102] You, on the other hand, are naming more than just a baby — you're naming an entire revolution of babies. Except they're grown up babies, also known as "adults." Think of your revolution as a group of babies, all waving torches and pitchforks, while chanting, "We shall overcome." This is how important this naming decision is. Also, nobody wants to see a baby get hurt.

Just imagine … you might be the one who comes up with the next great revolution name. Will you be the one who names the next Bolshevik Revolution, the next American Revolution, or even the beloved but short-lived one-hit wonder, Dexy's Midnight Runners Revolution? Only time

101. That solved everything.

102. Books.

103. Trust me,
time *always*
tells. It can't
keep a secret
to save its life.

will tell.[103] But how will you accomplish this? The following is a flowchart, which through a series of questions will lead you in determining the name of your revolution. Follow the flowchart from questions one through ten, to accurately determine what the name of *your* revolution should be.

THE REVOLUTION
NAMING FLOW CHART

I. Is your revolution male or female?

This is imperative, for knowing the gender of your revolution will allow you to determine whether its name should end in the masculine "o" or the feminine "a." If your revolution is transgendered, or Italian, then its name should end in "i."

2. Is this a good revolution or a bad revolution?

You wouldn't conduct business with a witch if you didn't know whether she was good or bad, and for the same reason you shouldn't name a revolution if you don't know in which direction points its moral compass. Good revolutions generally have shorter names, whereas bad revolutions usually have longer names.

3. Is there room for irony in your revolution?

Those in the mafia often receive ironic nicknames that refer to a particular physical characteristic — such as "Little" Tony, "Really Good Looking" Steve or "Hope You Don't Mind That I'm Not Italian" Mario. While the same principle can be applied to revolutions, it must be done skillfully. The "Deathless Revolution" is a funny and ironic name, because more than 100,000 people died as a result.[104] The "Efficient Revolution" however does not work as a functional name, because nobody thinks it's funny that the revolution took more than 27 years to occur, and required a lot of paperwork.

104. Comedygold™

4. What kind of mood is your revolution in?

Will people involved in your revolution be fighting? Reading documents? Singing and dancing? Watching television? More specifically, *what will be their mood?* Knowing the mood of your revolution can help you determine the name. For example, the "Green Revolution" can represent those who care about the environment *and* those who are quite jealous.[105]

105. Of the environment.

6.) Are you opposed to using the word "blood" in your revolution? What about the words "buckets of?"

Just checking.

7. What about numbers?

While numbers are often dismissed as being clichéd, boring, and overused, numbers can actually add zest to any naming situation. Consider, for example, the "War of 1812." While on the surface it appears to be a bland war, the number 1812 actually has a double meaning: 1812 is both the year the war took place, and is also the number of Canadian troops who died in battle after getting dysentery. This is why most Canadians avoid the year 1812 whenever possible.[106]

106. As well as February.

8. Is your revolution of royal lineage?

A great religious philosopher once said, "Do not cast pearls before swine, because when was the last time you saw a pig wearing a necklace?" Although your revolution might not technically be a pig, the principle still applies. Who is carrying out your revolution? If it consists primarily of royalty and the upper class, then you want a revolution that reflects that status — such as "The Gold Standard Revolution" or "Platinum Card Revolution." If those involved with your revolution are of the middle or lower class, then any boring word will do.[107]

107. Like "potato" or "Roseanne marathon."

9. Is your revolution carbon neutral?

It is imperative that you determine the carbon neutrality of your revolution before choosing a name. Why is this important? Should your revolution not be carbon neutral, you will then be required to choose an environmentally friendly name to offset your revolution's carbon footprint. For example: the "Green Revolution." Or the "Tree Hugger Revolution." Or the "Birkenstock Wearing Revolution." Or the "Every Time Al Gore Farts, Another Tree is Planted Revolution." All of these names will offset your revolution's carbon emissions.

10. Does your revolution have an acceptable credit score?

You may think that a credit score doesn't matter, but what you don't realize is that someday, you're going to want to buy a house. If your revolution has defaulted on credit cards, declared bankruptcy, or changed its name in an attempt at hiding from a past checkered with forged checks,[108] then it is unlikely that the banks will approve of a high-credit name. Names usually approved include the "Cash Advance Revolution," or the "Financial Solvency Revolution." Those with a low credit score should still keep to more

108. Is it possible that your revolution is actually Frank Abagnale in disguise?

appropriate names, such as the "Payday Loan Revolution," or the "Gary Coleman Revolution."

CONGRATULATIONS! Write the name of your new revolution here:

_____

DECIDING ON YOUR REVOLUTIONARY SLOGAN

Quick, name the first thing that comes into your head when you hear "Snap, Crackle, Pop." You thought of guerilla warfare, right? Now complete the following advertisement jingle: "The best part of waking up is _____." Did you come up with "The best part of waking up is *knowing you weren't viciously beaten to death in your sleep*?" Correct again. Now name the product that this slogan is advertising: "Obey Your Thirst." Did you guess "Sprite?" Well, you're wrong. The right answer was "Ruthless Communist Despot."

The human brain is a curious thing, and for that reason, it can be tricked to believe anything we want it to believe. Do you want people to visit your pizza parlor, donate to your political candidate, or drink your poisoned Kool-Aid?[109] Trick the human brain with *slogans* and *mottos*. We are conditioned to obey catchy jingles and witty phrases, and will buy every idea, Coke, and feminine hygiene product thrown at us. Why not apply the same principle to your revolution?[110]

You've come up with a powerful, but efficient, but succinct, but jazzy name for your revolution. All you need is an accompanying slogan or motto. However, perhaps you think that having a slogan is trivial, and only necessary for cigar-smoking Madison Avenue fat cats looking to make a quick buck. And that's not you — you're a rebel, you're a maverick, and you don't fit in a box! Well, I have news for you.[111] Underestimating the importance of a slogan or

109. C'mon, it's grape flavored!

110. Yeah, why not?

111. Listen up!

motto is something you do at your own peril, for many a guillotine has fallen over the head of the revolutionary who put "find a slogan" on his to-do list below "do laundry," "mow the lawn," and "avoid being beheaded."

Before constructing your own slogans and mottos, it is important that you learn about past slogans throughout history that have been used in revolutions. As you will see, not one single slogan is perfect, as they all have their pros and cons. It's also important that you learn which slogans are dairy-based, in case you're lactose-intolerant. Although let's be honest — if you're lactose-intolerant, you have no business being a revolutionary in the first place.[112]

112. Same goes for wheat allergies.

"All power to the Soviets."	
This slogan is taken from the October Revolution.	
PRO: The slogan clearly outlines who will be receiving all power.	**CON:** The slogan doesn't specify what *kind* of power. Invisibility? Flying? Laser eyes?

"Democracy is the best revenge."	
This is a general slogan relating to revolutions that promote democracy.	
PRO: As this slogan points out, why use violence, when you can use voting and congressmen?	**CON:** Everyone knows that "revenge is a dish best served cold." But it's also true that "Democracy is the best revenge." Therefore, should we assume that Antarctica is the birthplace of democracy? Yes, we should.

"Don't tread on me."

Used during the American Revolution, this slogan is traced to publications by Benjamin Franklin.

PRO: This slogan invokes imagery of a poisonous snake, which can instill fear into your enemies' hearts.	**CON:** Snakes can be killed with a hoe, or snake poison, and then how ridiculous will you look with a dead snake as your revolutionary slogan? Answer: very.

"End the war in Vietnam. Bring our troops home now!"

This was the primary slogan used by anti-war activists during the Vietnam War.

PRO: A powerful slogan, as it serves a dual purpose — fighting for both the end of a war, and bringing home the troops.	**CON:** This slogan is too long. As pointed out earlier, most revolutionaries have short attention spans. I feel asleep half way through this slogan.

"Gentlemen, you can't fight in here! This is the War Room."

This revolutionary slogan is from the film *Dr. Strangelove*.

PRO: Although a somewhat enigmatic slogan, this at least informs revolutionaries where they can and cannot fight.	**CON:** If you can't fight in the war room, then what's the pointing in having one? Where else is a revolutionary going to fight — in the parlor? Let's not be ridiculous. What is a parlor?

"Give me liberty or give me death."

This famous slogan by Patrick Henry is from the American Revolution.

PRO: This slogan is very force-ful, as it puts the revolutionary's life on the line for a belief in liberty.	**CON:** Giving enemies the choice of giving you death means you will probably die. A more effective slogan would be "Give me liberty or give me a mean scowl."

"I choo-choo-choose you."

This slogan is taken from an episode of a revolutionary show known as *The Simpsons*.

PRO: Generations of revolutionaries have been inspired by this slogan, knowing that they were cho-cho-chosen by a higher power to overthrow the government.	**CON:** Sure, it's cute. But maybe a little too cute.

"If war is the answer, we're asking the wrong question."

This is another slogan often used by peace activists.

PRO: A clever slogan, as this subtly moves the emphasis away from war, and provides an alternative as the 'answer.'	**CON:** If you're asking the wrong question, then perhaps you should focus on asking the correct one.[113] I'm not one to tell you what the correct question would be, but I will tell you that it begins with "how much wood" and ends with "if a woodchuck could chuck wood?"

113. Can I have "What are we fighting for?" for $200, Alex?

"No taxation without representative."

This well-known slogan is from the American Revolution.

PRO: This slogan is forceful, it rhymes, and it clearly lays out what the revolutionary is seeking.	**CON:** Really? Protesting taxes? What's next — are you going to get all fired up over the skyrocketing price of lip balm? It should be pointed out that nothing worthwhile has ever come from revolting over taxes.

"Our movement is Hosseini, our leader is Khomein!"

This slogan is from the Iranian Revolution.

PRO: This is an effective slogan, as it clearly defines both the movement and the revolution's leader.	**CON:** "Hosseini" doesn't exactly roll off your tongue. But that's because your tongue's been cut off. Because you're an infidel.

"Peace, bread and land."

The October Revolution was the inspiration for this particular slogan.

PRO: While many slogans from revolutions and protests invoke violence, this on the other hand invokes peace and prosperity.	**CON:** What if you're not in the mood for bread? What if you want a cobb salad or a grilled chicken parmesan sandwich or something?

"Power to the people."

Taken from a song by John Lennon, this slogan inspires civil disobedience.

PRO: Not only is this slogan succinct yet powerful, but it is also the quintessential slogan of the proletariat.

CON: As we learned from the film *Spiderman*, with great power comes great responsibility. And let's be honest — power to the people is a nice idea, but probably shouldn't go to all people.
Do we really want powerful drug dealers? Or powerful zamboni drivers? Or powerful actors in a community theatre version of *Starlight Express*? I think we all know the answer to that question.

"Release the secret weapon."

This slogan is from the animated film, *An American Tail*.

PRO: This slogan, when chanted by groups of revolutionaries, informs all that freedom will be acquired by means of releasing a secret weapon.

CON: Not only are there cats in America, but the streets are most certainly not paved in cheese. What a load of bullshit.

"Sometimes you feel like a nut, sometimes you don't."

This revolutionary slogan is from the Mounds candy bar.

PRO: Almond Joy's got nuts.

CON: Mounds don't.

"The British are coming!"

A phrase shouted by Paul Revere during the American Revolution.

PRO: A slogan learned by all American elementary students, this is quite effectual as it prepares the revolutionary for the approaching enemy.	**CON:** Most people now assume this slogan relates to the deluge of British television shows that have been adapted for American audiences. And they're right.

"United we stand, divided we fall."

This slogan was common during the American Revolution.

PRO: This powerful slogan has been adapted by many causes, beliefs, and protests, and can be used for a wide variety of revolutions.	**CON:** While unity is usually preferred, dividing yourself from members of your revolution is sometimes suggested. Like, for example, if you have leprosy.

"Viva la revolucion!"

This slogan is taken from the Cuban Revolution.

PRO: Although originally spoken in Spanish, this generic slogan can be used for a wide variety of revolutions.	**CON:** A common mistake when employing this slogan is to confuse it with, "Viva Las Vegas." On more than one occasion, there has been a revolutionary who accidentally shouted "Viva la revolucion," only to wake up in the morning broke, with a hangover, and married to stranger who happens to be a showgirl.

"Votes for women."

This slogan was used during the Women's Suffrage movement.

PRO: A very effective slogan, as it's clear, concise, and direct.	CON: The idea of trading votes for women is a very offensive idea. Women are not commodities to be bartered with or traded. Votes for bribes? Perhaps. But votes for women? Absolutely not.

"Voting is the right that protects all other rights."

This slogan is popular in protests that promote voting rights and democracy.

PRO: A great slogan, as it really drives home the importance of voting as a tool of democracy.	CON: Voting may be the right that protects all other rights, but who's going to protect Voting? Hopefully Voting carries a gun or knows self-defense. On second thought, it's probably better that Voting just not leave the house after dark.

"War is expensive, peace is priceless."

This slogan is used by peace activists who are revolting against war.

PRO: This is an optimistic slogan, contrasting war with the preferred goal of obtaining peace.	CON: Actually, peace is not priceless, as it currently carries a retail price of $4.95, plus shipping and handling.

"Well-behaved women rarely make history."

This slogan of the Women's Rights movement is from Laurel Thatcher Ulrich.

PRO: This is a great slogan, because it promotes the idea that civil disobedience leads to progress.

CON: Unfortunately, this slogan isn't entirely true. For example, Mattie Goldberg made history for being the first woman in a wheelchair to win the "Most Well Behaved Woman" contest back in 1987.

"We're here, we're queer, get used to it."

This slogan is from the Gay Rights movement.

PRO: This slogan reiterates the gay community's determination to be accepted into mainstream society like everyone else.

CON: All that talent in the gay community, and this is the best they could come up with? They've had everyone from Freddie Mercury to Elton John to Boy George — and they couldn't even come up with a slogan that rhymes? Not even "We're gay, we'll be here everyday?"[114] Or "We're homo, and that doesn't blow?"[115] What about "We don't need to be straight, 'cause we don't want to mate?"[116]

"Who would Jesus bomb?"

This revolutionary slogan is occasionally used by anti-war activists.

PRO: This puts a clever twist on the well-known slogan, "What Would Jesus Do?"

CON: Answer: Jesus would bomb abortion clinics.

114. Patent pending.
115. Patent pending.
116. Patent pending.

BUILD YOUR OWN REVOLUTIONARY SLOGAN

You've watched on the sidelines for long enough. It's now time for you to get into the game. The slogan-building game. And yes, I know what you're thinking: you finally have an excuse to wear those shoulder pads.[117]

The following is a diagram, which will help you construct your own revolutionary slogan or motto. Simply choose a phrase from Column A, followed by Column B, and finish with Column C. Feel free to mix and match until you find the slogan that best fits the needs of your revolution.

117. I'm going to ignore the fact that you're already wearing the jock strap.

Column A	Column B	Column C
Fight	the tyrants until they become	the vanquished.
We are	the Champions of	the World.
Down with the	the bastards, and up with	common sense.
War is	expensive, peace is	priceless.
Stick it to	the Man and	the Woman.
We are for	a worker's republic, not	a bourgeois republic.
Go for	the gold, and never settle for	second place.
Life,	Liberty, and the pursuit of	happiness.
I'm mad as	hell, and I'm not going to take	this anymore!
We demand	equal rights, and won't settle for	anything else.
M&Ms melt	in your mouth, and not it	your hand.
Peace is	the light, the way, and is	the Lord.
You gotta fight, for	your right, to	party.
Voting is	a privilege that belongs to	everybody.
Life is like	a box of chocolates, you never know	what you're going to get.
The power is	within	all of us.
Money is	the root of	all evil.
We're here, we're	queer, get used to	it.

The following is a list of examples that I came up with, using this diagram. Feel free to use any of these, or come up with your own:

- The power is the gold, and never settle for the Lord.
- We demand the bastards, and up with all evil.
- Money is queer, get used to second place.
- Voting is a box of chocolates, you never know happiness.
- Fight a privilege that belongs to the Woman.
- We're here, we're the root of your hand.
- You gotta fight, for the Champions of anything else.
- Peace is in your mouth, and not in a bourgeois republic.

A REVOLUTIONARY FUN FACT!

Approximately 74 percent of all slogans or mottos used in revolutions consist of a noun, a verb, a past participle, and a generic cream cheese filling.

A LAST WORD: DOES YOUR REVOLUTION NEED A CHANT?

Everybody needs a *butcher*. We have to eat and — with the exception of vegetarians, vegans, and supermodels — meat will always be part of a regular diet. Everybody also needs a *baker*. Bread is delicious, especially when it's made from cinnamon and raisins and warm and drizzled with honey. It's like the nectar of the Gods, but instead of nectar, it's bread. But do you know what nobody needs? A *candlestick maker.* Who uses candles these days? Nobody, that's who.[118]

Just as we need a butcher, a baker, and *not* a candlestick maker, does the modern revolutionary need a name, a slogan, and *not* a chant. A revolutionary chant is as useless as a candlestick maker, or a wallet with no money, or a nose ring. You should think of all these different pieces — the name, slogan and chant — as a family. If revolutionary songs are the *father* and revolutionary slogans are the *mother*, then revolutionary chants are the *red-headed step-child*. Why are revolutionary chants red-headed? Because they're wearing a wig. It's not a great wig, but at least it covers up the fact that revolutionary chants are going bald. Unfortunately, a wig can't cover up the fact that revolutionary chants are adopted.

From a third world country.

Now clearly I have a strong opinion against chants. This is for one reason and one reason only: *They rarely work.* Second reason: *they make you sound like you're in musical theater.* Repetitively chanting "Hell no, we won't go" or "We want fairer wages" may sound assertive and committed, but the truth is, it makes you sound as if you're auditioning for *Les Miserable*. While dressed like a 17th-century dandy. Plus, you're holding a puppy.[119]

Yes, it's true that chanting and trumpet-playing brought down the walls of Jericho. But do you know what the walls of Jericho were made of during the days of the Bible? Straw, prayers to Jehovah, and horse dung. Do you know what we make our walls out of today? Steel, concrete, and kryptonite. Chanting may have worked during the Old Testament, but these days if you want to take down a wall, you need something that's slightly more heavy-duty than a measly chant. Like a wrecking ball.[120]

Being full of rage and ferocity is great, but it's best to channel such anger into something more effective than a sing-songy chant. Try throwing a Molotov cocktail into a group of innocent bystanders. Try screaming while thrusting torches and pitchforks into the air as if you're drunk. Try getting mad as hell and not taking it anymore, by signing a petition with a mean look in your eye. But if at all possible, avoid chanting. Nobody takes chants seriously. Chanting adds unnecessary frivolity and mirth to a revolution — and if there's one thing a revolutionary needs more than anything else, it's to be taken seriously.

Also, clown costumes are frowned upon.[121]

120. Horse dung mixed with fuel oil will also work.

121. Unless it's a *menacing* clown costume.

IN THEIR OWN REVOLUTIONARY WORDS

"Nonviolence is not inaction. It is not for the timid or the weak. It is hard work; it is the patience to win. And anyone who disagrees with me can tell my fists."

CESAR CHAVEZ
Labor Leader and civil rights activist

6

from pamphleteering to posting humiliating personal ads: how to recruit for your revolution

Revolutions are like a game of chess. Like chess, revolutions require many individuals in order to defeat a foe. The pawns, bishops, knights, and queens in chess are the peasant boys, clergymen, weight lifters, and drag queens of a revolution. Also, revolutions occasionally take place on a checkered board, just like chess. Revolutions sometimes use small pieces carved out of marble, just like chess. Revolutions are frequently played in the park with a homeless man named Clive who talks to himself, just like chess. In fact, revolutions are sometimes even won by Bobby Fischer,[122] just like chess.

You're not going to win an entire chess game with just one chess piece (unless it's a queen[123]), and you're certainly not going to win a revolution with just one person (unless it's a really strong and intelligent person with the ability to be many places at once[124]). You need people on your side: dedicated combatants and followers who will carry out your political goals and ambitions. If overthrowing the government is your goal, then many hands will be required.[125] Only those who have the cooperation of many people's hands, or the Hindu goddess Kali, will be successful.

Where will you find these people, willing to join your cause? Do you post a listing on Craigslist? Do you send out homing pigeons to various cities across the Midwest? Do you tag rest stop bathrooms with your ex-girlfriend's phone number and the message, "For a good, time call?" Do you give free tiny bottles of gin to alcoholics, with a secret message rolled up inside? Do you pay hobo children a farthing to spread the good news of your revolution as they ride trains across America, on their way to the Annual Hobo Jubilee?

Yes.

Recruiting people for your revolution requires creativity, tenacity, and a court-ordered week in AA. You may have to search for people in very unsavory places, such as hippie communes, or Quebec, Canada. Unfortunately, potential revolutionaries don't just wave a flag and reveal themselves to you. Thus, you must be cunning, observe human behavior,

122. Oh, there he is!

123. Or you're cheating.

124. Or you're cheating.

125. Preferably, still attached to people.

and wear X-ray glasses. It also helps to wear camouflage, so that you blend in. You wouldn't visit an elementary school, a public execution, or a Cinnabon without wearing a helmet, would you? For these same reasons, you should not attempt to recruit for your revolution if you're not wearing camouflage.

Are you prepared for some rough and ready recruiting? Or some soft and unprepared recruiting? Either way, the following list will serve as a jumping off point.

IN THEIR OWN REVOLUTIONARY WORDS

"I am going to fight capitalism even if it kills me. It is wrong that people like you should be comfortable and well fed while all around you people are starving. But it's a great way to lose weight!"

SYLVIA PANKHURST
*British suffragette campaigner
and communist*

WHERE DO YOU FIND PEOPLE FOR YOUR REVOLUTION?

Universities, Colleges, and Technical Schools for the "Gifted"

These are some of the best places to find revolutionaries, as most students have very impressionable minds, ready to be molded so that they might follow your every injunction. While most universities and colleges are ripe with recruits, you would be wise to avoid schools whose mascot is a cougar, schools founded by the Illuminati, and schools who don't offer at least a Master's degree in mixology.

Churches, Synagogues, and Temples

Attending a house of worship requires *faith*. Having *faith* is to have the confident belief in the truth of a person, idea, or thing without the presence of substantial proof. There is a *country* singer named *Faith* Hill. This *country* was founded in 1776, thanks to the *American Revolution*. Ergo, *American Revolutionary* Benjamin Franklin accidentally discovered religion in his garage as a byproduct while inventing the bifocals [126] and listening to country music.

126. Bifocals, for those who aren't familiar, swing both ways

Arts Festivals and Music Festivals

Such festivals usually tend to be filled with hippies, anarchists, and others who are liberally minded. If you make it past these people, you'll end up finding recruits with actual potential.

Libraries

People who frequent libraries generally have two great loves: great literature, and slashing throats. Think about it.[127]

127. J.K. Rowling?

Abortion Clinics

This is a great place to find recruits for your revolution, since the type of people who get abortions are usually the type of people who would join a political revolution. Plus, you probably won't want a baby hanging around a revolution anyway, so abortion clinics serve a dual purpose.[128]

128. Have you ever noticed that most abortion doctors hate babysitting?

Truck Stops

As it turns out, truck stops are ideal places to meet people willing to join your revolution. Truck drivers, due to the ebb and flow of their chosen profession, understand human nature, as well as how to bring down the entire network upon which rests a nation.

Bonus: Truck stops are also great places to have anonymous gay sex.[129]

129. So … I've heard.

Inside the Whale That Swallowed Jonah

This may seem like an odd place to find potential revolutionaries, but trust me — Jonah will join your movement, no matter what the cause. It's not like he has anything else to do.[130]

130. Well, aside from Sudoku.

Fat Camp

Let's be honest: nobody at fat camp actually wants to be there.[131] By breaking people out of fat camp and asking them to join your revolution, you do both of yourselves a favor — they get to escape, and you have new recruits!

But first, they're going to have to lose some weight.

131. See movie; *Heavy Weights*, (1995) directed by Steven Brill.

Bar, Pubs, and Taverns

Surprisingly, your local bar or pub is a great location when searching for those willing to join your revolution. Not only are such drinking establishments filled with people ready to be manipulated, but odds are that if you buy the next pitcher, they'll offer to die for your cause. And then throw up all over your new pantsuit.

Cemeteries

You might not think that a cemetery would be an ideal place to recruit potential revolutionaries, but let me propose the following question: who's going to try to kill a ghost? Nobody, that's who.

Strip Clubs

Why are stripper clubs good places to recruit revolutionaries, you may ask? Strippers use greased up poles ... revolutionaries use greased up poles ... I think you see where I'm going with this.[132]

132. I sure don't.

The Children's Television Workshop

The people who write for children's television, such as Sesame Street, are already used to having blood on their hands. Being a revolutionary isn't that big of a stretch.[133]

133. Little known revolutionary fact: Elmo is a former Zapatista.

On a Train

A train! A train! Could you recruit, would you recruit, on a train? Not in a train! Not in a tree! Not in a car! Sam! Let me be!

No, seriously. You really need to learn personal boundaries.

At the base of the Christ the Redeemer statue in Rio de Janeiro, Brazil.

No one exactly knows why, but revolutionaries tend to be fascinated by grotesquely oversized statues of Jesus Christ. So, jack pot.

A Cabbage Patch

It's well known that cabbage patches are useful for just three reasons: finding potential revolutionaries, finding creepy dolls with round heads, and finding children raised from the dead who will go on a murder spree. Try to avoid the later two.

Alcoholics Anonymous Meetings

The benefit of finding potential revolutionaries at an Alcoholic Anonymous meeting is that it's one of the few places where God will grant you the serenity to accept the things you cannot change, courage to change the things you can, and wisdom to know the difference. Plus, people recruited at Alcoholics Anonymous meetings always know where the best bars are.[134]

134. So …
I've heard.

The Fountain of Youth

Consider this: those who spend time at the Fountain of Youth are filled with a renewed lease on life, having recently acquired the priceless gift of immortality. Therefore it is these people whom you want in your revolution. The tricky part, of course, is finding the Fountain of Youth.

Taking Interstate 80, you're going to head west until you reach Highway 101, at which point you're going to head south. You'll take the third exit and pass some construction, which means you're heading the right way. After you go through five traffic lights, one of which will be broken, you'll turn left and pass a gas station with a weird colored roof. Apparently it had some rain damage or something.

Head about ten more miles until you see a large barn that has been tagged with Masonic graffiti. Turn right at the fork in the road. After a few more minutes you're going to come across a tree that looks similar to character actor Harry Dean Stanton. Take the dirt road that is right after the tree. After a few hours you'll come to the Fountain of Youth.

If you pass a Wal-Mart, you've gone too far.

Annual Revolutionary Convention

Surprisingly, there are always lots of good recruits — as well as theme ideas — at the Annual Revolutionary Convention, held next year in St. Louis, Missouri. Be sure to visit me at booth #1731, and ask for your free keychain![135]

Places you should absolutely avoid when recruiting for your revolution include:

- Unemployment offices
- Tattoo parlors
- Inside a slightly used tauntaun from the ice planet Hoth
- Used car lots
- Nurseries (both babies and plants)
- The ruins of Machu Picchu
- See's Candies stores
- The 1960s
- The sky, as you're skydiving
- Mt. Rushmore (specifically, noses)
- Applebee's

135. That will be $3.99.

- 300 kilometers off the coast of Easter Island, in any direction
- The inside of an empty barrel that was once filled with memories
- Scottsdale, Arizona

A REVOLUTIONARY FUN FACT!

The Centrella Bed & Breakfast Inn in Monterey, California is the most romantic place in the world to recruit revolutionaries for your bloody coup d'état.

Be sure to ask for the Lovebirds Discount. It includes a complimentary bottle of champagne … and his-and-hers semi-automatic rifles!

HOW TO FIND
REVOLUTIONARIES ONLINE

What a glorious age of technology we live in! Between computers, telephones, the pony express, and vegetable oil-powered zeppelins carrying birthday croissants and walkie-talkies, sharing communication between adults[136] has never been faster or more efficient. More specifically, our generation has been the first to use the Internet to spread knowledge, ideas, porn, and crippling computer viruses. Can you imagine spreading a crippling computer virus using nothing more than a horse and buggy? You should — because that's what they did during the late 1800s![137]

136. And sometimes children, depending on the laws in your state.

137. As well as during a 15-minute period in 1974.

Is finding recruits for your revolution online a good idea? Of course it is! Recruiters for modeling agencies, the military, polygamist compounds, and Haiti have found success over the years using a combination of both offline and online methods. You're not about to be called "antiquated" by a Haitian polygamist, are you? If you wish to be a modern revolutionary, then you must employ modern tactics. Now obviously you're going to have a lot of questions, such as:

• How do you recruit people on the Internet?

• What are the best Web sites to use?

• Spam e-mail about penile dysfunction: good idea or great idea?

• Will watching a viral video of a penguin getting hit by a car get you arrested? (answer: probably yes)

• You know what's really boring? Books.[138]

• Also: using a computer too much will cause you to die from which of the following — plane crash or herpes?

The World Wide Web is extremely large (but ironically, not that wide), and so it's easy to see how some may feel intimidated to jump in headfirst. This is why I've prepared the following list of Web sites you can use to recruit people for your revolution. Due to the fact that many Web sites are connected to others via links (creating a "web," if you will), I've also included a list of Web sites you should explicitly avoid at all costs.

138. Except for this book, which is entertaining and enlightening and everyone should own three copies.

Websites You Should Use

CRAIGSLIST.ORG: This is the grandpappy of online classified ads, and was the inspiration behind both the penny-saver of the 1940s, and Finland. Although it tends to be swarmed by spammers and those who don't know how to spell, Craigslist continues to be a great place to post ads for revolutionaries, especially if they're for sale.

TWITTER.COM: If you can say it in 140 characters, you can say it in 100 characters. And if you can say it in 100 characters, then it will probably fit inside a breadbox. Do you know what else fits inside a breadbox? Midgets. And every revolution needs at least one midget to squeeze into those hard to fit places.[139]

WIKIPEDIA.ORG: One of the most amazing things about Wikipedia, aside from the free burro rides, is that it was the first encyclopedia in history with the ability to be written and rewritten and rerewritten. This of course raises an important question: if an online encyclopedia can change how history is remembered, does that mean that history itself has changed (via DeLorean)? Yes, of course. And who is it that's responsible for changing history? Marty McFly. And revolutionaries. Hence, you will find revolutionaries on Wikipedia.

FANDANGO.COM: Movies are the window to the soul of the human race. Any Web site that allows the human race to purchase movie tickets at an inflated ticket price is a Web site that is used by the best and the brightest humanity has to offer. Therefore, anyone who is reckless enough to consciously pay a $2 to $3 surcharge is someone you want for your revolution.

WEB MD.COM: Everyone gets sick at some point in their lives (well, with the exception of doctors, which is why they became doctors in the first place). Why not recruit potential revolutionaries when they're not feeling well and are at their most vulnerable? Same principle applies to people at church or watching *The Bridges of Madison County*.

YOUTUBE.COM: One of the most selfless acts a person could possibly do, aside from giving his or her life for their country, is to spend hours watching video clips of piano playing kittens, commercial parodies, twelve-year-olds with high pitched voices, news anchors stumbling over their words, and farting babies. Anyone who has that kind of time is usually willing to die for a great political cause and/or should die anyway.

139. And to kick ankles.

Web sites You Should Not Use

FACEBOOK.COM: As the saying goes, "Don't eat in the same place where you defecate." While it may be exciting to find childhood friends on Facebook, it doesn't necessarily mean they'll be willing to die for your political cause. Unless of course, you tag them in a picture.

EBAY.COM: This online auction site is very useful for many things: completing your antique Pez collection, finding platform shoes that once belonged to Gary Coleman, and selling all of your ex-girlfriend's material goods without her knowledge. Unfortunately, eBay is not very useful when it comes to finding revolutionaries, due to the fact that the Web site is heavily regulated. In fact, eBay is so regulated, the FCC once fined Janet Jackson for selling a piece of her malfunctioning wardrobe.

GMAIL.COM: One of the most heavily used services in the world, Gmail allows users to send "emails," which is short for "emai. letters." Although the service — which is owned by Google — is well known, nobody actually knows what the "G" in "Gmail" stands for. Government-mail? Glengarry-Glen-Ross-mail? Gonna-kill-all-revolutionaries-mail? If you can't trust Gmail, you can't trust the people who use it. Don't use it to find your revolutionaries.

NETFLIX.COM: Netflix is a groundbreaking online movie rental service, which made history for being the first company to give away DVDs in red envelopes during Chinese weddings. The Chinese may argue that this idea was ripped off from the centuries old Chinese custom, but then again, Mao Zedong lead the Cultural Revolution in China, and look what happened to him. He's dead. Is it a coincidence that Mao Zedong died in 1976, the same year that Netflix wasn't incorporated? I rest my case.

CNN.COM: Sure, this Web site may tout itself as the "most trusted name in news" and "a Web site," but that doesn't necessarily mean that it doesn't have an agenda. CNN survives because it owes money to advertisers and rich muckie mucks, and they dislike anyone who disrupts their nightly dosage of Levitra ads. You may not find revolutionaries at CNN.com, but you will find stuffed shirts and erectile dysfunction.

? A REVOLUTIONARY QUIZ ?

Which of the following popular vacation destinations is the best city to recruit for your revolution:

A) Las Vegas, Nevada — "Sin City":
Residents of Las Vegas play fast and loose with money, alcohol, and women, and aren't afraid to take risks. Someone who's not afraid to lose everything to gain anything is someone you want for your revolution.

B) New York City, New York — "The Big Apple":
New Yorkers are known for their steely resolve, as it takes a lot to disturb their way of life. Someone with that kind of grit is someone you want for your revolution.

C) Chicago, Illinois — "The Second City":
Whether producing a U.S. President or a family of mayors, Chicago is known for being a political factory. A city with that kind of dedication to civics will produce someone you want for your revolution.

D) Newark, New Jersey — "A City in New Jersey":
We're not sure how we ended up here, but do you mind just giving us directions to get back on the freeway?

HOW TO CONVINCE PEOPLE TO JOIN YOUR REVOLUTION

Let's say a stranger walked up to you and asked you to give him all your money. While your initial reaction might be to not cooperate, odds are that you would eventually give in to such demands. What exactly was it that caused you to change your mind? Was it his soothing voice? Was it his promises of a better life? Or was it the fact that the stranger pointed a loaded revolver to your head? This leads us to the next logical question: what exactly was the loaded revolver loaded *with*? Pudding? Marbles? Good feelings? Bullets? How about *vanilla* pudding? Regardless of how he convinced you, the one thing the stranger did do was acquire your money through *coercion*.

Coercion?[140]

"Coercion" may be a nasty word (because it never washes its hands after using the bathroom), but it is nevertheless an essential tool for any revolutionary who wishes to recruit people to join his or her cause. You may know where to find your potential revolutionaries, but unfortunately, this is only the beginning.[141] You can't just show up with arms open, ready to recruit, and expect revolutionaries to jump into your arms with reckless abandon. Revolutionaries have to be *coerced* into joining. You've heard of the saying "You can lead a horse to water, but you can't make it drink." The reason it can't drink is because the water is polluted — and who wants a horse with jaundice?

140. Yes, coercion.

141. You may have noticed by this point that I've mentioned a number of times that you're "only beginning" to be a revolutionary. Don't you feel frustrated that you've reached Chapter 6 and you're *still* "only beginning?" Personally, I think you should stop asking questions and pay attention to the road. Also, why are you reading this book while driving?

It's worth pointing out that coercion isn't necessarily a bad thing. Like "love" or "declaring bankruptcy," it can be both good or bad, depending on the situation and the time of year (for example: wedding season). The following are some of the more effective methods of coercion to recruit revolutionaries.

NOTE: If, after exhausting all of the following methods, you find yourself lacking in revolutionaries, do not hesitate to resort to kidnapping and/or cupcakes. Why cupcakes, you ask? Because after kidnapping someone, you may want a tasty snack.

COERCIVE TECHNIQUES

MONEY/BRIBES

The time-honored tradition of bribing people to join your cause is as old as time itself, going back to at least the 1970s. Although paying cash is preferable over a check, a bribe can still be paid by check as long as you cross out your name and don't sign at the bottom. Where it says "Memo," you'll want to write "Not for a revolution." Contrary to what you've seen in the movies, do not, under any circumstances, give someone a stack of $2 bills as a bribe. Those are collectable.

FRUIT BASKETS

Receiving a fruit basket from someone is akin to receiving a basket full of sunshine, happiness, and fruit. It brightens up the day, and inspires the recipient to get all political. Be sure to avoid giving a basket with *rotten* fruit, as anyone receiving a moldy fruit basket will take that as a threat. Then again, threats are *also* considered coercion, so it's a win-win situation either way.

VIOLENT THREATS

Remember how your mother used to tell you "Always wear clean underwear because you never know when you'll go to the hospital; and also always keep a metal bat in the trunk of your car, because you never know when you'll need to threaten someone." Well, your mother was right. Violent threats always work when recruiting people. But only if you're wearing clean underwear. You don't want the last thought going through someone's head as you crack a metal bat over the skull to be, "Didn't his mother raise him correctly?"

GIFT CERTIFICATES

What, you think those $25 gift certificates to Outback Steakhouse are just going to give *themselves* away? You want revolutionary warriors — and revolutionary warriors want a Blooming Onion — so why not kill two birds with one stone? But how exactly will you use just *one* stone to kill *two* birds? Answer: *a boomerang-shaped stone*. And where do you find a boomerang-shaped stone? Answer: at an Australian-themed chain restaurant. Or at Outback Steakhouse.

BLACKMAIL

It's surprising that more people don't engage in blackmail, due to the fact that it's incredibly easy and hassle-free. Pre-developed blackmail pictures are available almost everywhere these days, ranging from Walgreens to Washington DC (in both cases, they're in the aisle next to the greeting cards). Many famous revolutionaries have been pressured to join a political movement out of fear that salacious pictures would come to light. Thomas Jefferson, for example, joined the American Revolution to prevent pictures of him and Sally Hemings from being leaked to the celebrity blogs.

AN INSPIRING POEM

People often underestimate the power of an inspiring poem, and do so at their own peril. Whether it be a sonnet about a midsummer night's dream, or a limerick about a man from Nantucket who did something incredibly inappropriate,[142] poems have inspired many revolutionaries to pick up a sword and a bookmark (so as not to lose their place in their poetry book). All types of poems are effective except for haikus, because syllable patterns of 5, 7, 5 are unnatural. Everyone knows that.

142. Hint: it rhymes with "Nantucket."

TORTURE

Telling someone you'll, "Beat you with a wet noodle," is funny. Telling someone, "And then I'll shove sharpened bamboo poles under your fingernails" is not funny. Telling someone, "And after the sharpened bamboo poles, I'm going to throw a cream pie in your face" *is absolutely hilarious*. Everyone may think they understand what 'torture' is, but the definition depends entirely on who's being asked. The next time somebody says, "The Geneva Conventions instructed us on how to treat people," remind them that the Geneva Conventions did not have any ice-breaker games, and the balloon drop in the ceiling completely malfunctioned. In other words, torture is totally fine.[143]

143. Unless it's happening to you.

EMPTY PROMISES

Everyone in life makes empty promises and says things they don't mean. "You're the best boss in the world," "You don't look fat in that dress," and "We've increased the ransom amount to $10 million dollars" are just a few that come to mind. Not surprisingly, these white lies and empty promises actually break down a person's will, to the point that they will do anything you desire. Ever promised a child that you would take him or her to Build-a-Bear, only to later inform the child that you made an even bigger promise to Johnnie Walker? Break enough promises, and eventually the child will do whatever you want: wash the dishes, mow the lawn, buy more Johnnie Walker, etc. Try the same idea with a budding revolutionary, and get the same results.

REALLY MEAN INSULTS

Let's say you're hypoglycemic. Do you want to be reminded that you're hypoglycemic? Of course not. Just imagine, then, if a guy wearing an eye patch and waving a flag which read "Free the Political Prisoners" walked up to you and called you a Hippo-glycemic-ugly. You would be offended, slightly confused, and at least slightly inquisitive about the eye patch. But would you join his movement to free the political prisoners? Of course you would. Does it matter what kind of political prisoners? Absolutely not. What does matter is that he deeply offended you, and the only way you can prove you're a man[144] is by donning the cape and joining his cause. By the way, the eye patch guy had a cape with him, in case you're wondering where the cape came from.

144. Unless you're a woman.

PANCAKES

Seriously, everybody loves pancakes.

A REVOLUTIONARY FUN FACT!

The Women's Suffrage Movement of the 1910s was sponsored by Trojan condoms.

7

speak softly and carry a big stick: or use your big boy words and not your fists

Congratulations. You've made it this far. You are now at the eleventh hour of the eleventh minute of the eleventh second of the eleventh whatever-comes-after-the-eleventh-second.[145] After all your preparation, you have finally reached the summit of the zenith of the apex, and as you stand at the pinnacle of your revolution, you may find yourself asking whether you've finally gotten over your acrophobia.[146] Now that you have all the ingredients for your revolution, you can bake it at 375° for half an hour, or until golden brown.[147] Be sure to

145. Twelve drummers drumming.

146. Acrophobia: "Fear of using a dictionary."

147. Unless you're on the raw food diet.

keep an eye on your baking revolution … nobody likes a burnt mixed metaphor!

I should point out that with the exception of chapters 2 and 5, this is the most important chapter in this book. In fact, I'll even go as far as to say that this is possibly the most important chapter in other books as well. For you see, it is this chapter that will provide you with the grassroots, down-in-the-dirt, tactical information you need, in order to rise up in one voice against your common enemy. And if no one else has joined your revolution and you find yourself absolutely and completely alone? Then it will be that much easier to rise up in one voice.

As you've learned throughout this book, there are as many types of revolutions as there are stars in the sky, or ways to skin a cat.[148] Some revolutions involve the slow march of progress, over time. Some involve the inevitable violence that follows the turnover of government. Some revolutions even require no purchase necessary (void where prohibited). Regardless of the differences in the many revolutions you will encounter, all eventually pass through three similar stages, or *intensity levels*, as described here:

148.
Seventeen.

Intensity Level 1 Letters & Petitions	Intensity Level 2 Protests & Rallies	Intensity Level 3 Riots & Violence

The first level in a revolution involves writing letters, signing petitions, general complaining, and other activities usually reserved for those who shout, "Get off my lawn, you damned kids," at the neighbors.

If this is ineffective in bringing about the desired change, the revolution then graduates to the second level, which involves protesting the targeted enemy and attending rallies (not to be confused with revolutionary prostitution or revolutionary drug dealing). Most revolutions spend the bulk of their time in this level, due to the fact that this level is usually where the best parties are (not to be confused with revolutionary prostitution or revolutionary drug dealing).

After protesting and rallying, many revolutions will then graduate to the last and most dramatic level: that of riots and violence. Although some revolutionaries (I'm looking at you, César Chávez!) believe that violence should be avoided at all costs, some revolutionaries understand that violence and punching is sometimes necessary to in order to accomplish one's goals. Writing letters may bring back a favorite but discontinued breakfast cereal, but rarely will letters depose the head of the government (unless a self-addressed stamped envelope is included).

Now of course some people may find themselves wondering how it is possible that something as complex as a political revolution can be shoehorned into three very specific, narrowly defined categories. After all, isn't life and human behavior so diverse and complicated that it would be naïve to believe that any kind of uprising could fit into only three simple levels of progression?

No.[149]

149. The simple answer is "no." The complex answer is "no," but with more words.

Even Revolutionaries Have Meetings

Meetings are an unpleasant fact of life. Unlike breathing, they are impossible to avoid. Even a chaotic revolution, with all its shouting, fighting, and down-the-stairs pushing,[150] requires a meeting to determine the logistics of when and where the down-the-stairs pushing will take place. Starting a revolution may at first appear to be all fun and games and beheadings, but the truth of the matter is that revolutions are all fun and games and *planning meetings*. Don't worry; most planning meetings include at least a few beheadings.

Unfortunately, even the simple task of holding a meeting for your revolution will become a challenge itself. Where do you meet? When is the best day for everyone? What if the authorities try to shut you down? Who provides the coffee and doughnuts?[151] Going from location to location in an attempt to hold your revolutionary meeting while running from authorities can feel like a game of Hot Potato, only without the aftertaste of sour cream and chives.

150. Now you know why 74 percent of all revolutionaries walk with a limp.

151. Usually Linda in accounting.

Obviously, the most important question to answer is *where* you should hold your planning meeting. Ideally, you want to find a versatile location, one that will provide ample space for battle plans, staff birthday parties, and cappuccino machines. A revolving bookcase leading to a dungeon is also a nice touch (although not necessary). What's important though is that your meeting be as clandestine as possible. Nearly everyone will want to shut down your revolution, including FBI agents, CIA agents, the local police, nosy dogs, old cranky men, Dennis the Menace, ghosts, zombies, the Jets (if you're a Shark), the Sharks (if you're a Jet), all the king's horses and all the king's men, and Eliot Ness.

Just as anyone buying a house understands that it's all about location, location, location, anyone holding a planning meeting for their revolution should understand it's all about privacy, privacy, privacy. If you happen to be a revolutionary realtor, then your main concern will be location, privacy, location, privacy, location, privacy.

Although technically a revolutionary meeting can be held anywhere, it is suggested that you use one of the following locations to plan your revolution.

Abandoned warehouses

This is a great location, as it is unlikely that anyone will come around to bother you. On the downside, you'll have to rotate every other week with the mob, depending on their schedule.

Community centers

Nobody ever thinks to check a community center for revolution planning meetings, because nobody ever visits a community center in the first place. In fact when I was much younger, there was a community center right around the corner from my house with a swimming pool and a gymnasium, and I don't think I even went once. Now to be fair, it may have had to do something with me being tiny and crippled, and always using crutches to get around. I remember one year, when Scrooge came over and picked me up, put me on his shoulders, and carried me around the house. That was the best Christmas ever. Too bad he was later arrested for being a pedophile.

Living rooms

Why not plan your revolution in somebody's living room? Sometimes the simplest idea is the best idea. Usually though, it is the very complicated idea that is even better. Having a meeting in someone's living room is comfortable, it's under the radar, and most living rooms even come equipped with a piano.[152] Family portrait sold separately.

152. Which makes the transition from "revolutionary planning meeting" to "old-fashioned piano party" that much easier.

The lobby of a bank

This may seem like an unlikely place to plan your revolution, as it is usually bustling with employees and bank customers. For that reason, it is completely unexpected. To get around any suspicion, it is suggested that you wear a facemask with holes cut out for the eyes and mouth, and run into the bank hurriedly. If you wave a gun while shouting at everyone, they will understand that you mean business and shouldn't be bothered.

The Louvre

Due to all the priceless art, nobody would ever think to find you planning your revolution at the Louvre. After hours, the museum is practically impenetrable. Unfortunately, you'll probably have a difficult time breaking in after hours, as apparently the museum is practically impenetrable (unproven).

A gym

Life is very busy these days, so why not combine your planning time with your workout time? A gym is one of the few places — with the exception of a Blockbuster video store[153] — where you can plan the takeover of the government *and* work on your hamstrings at the same time.

153. Just kidding, those don't exist anymore.

A china shop

Good place to meet. Unless you're a bull.

Arby's

Not only is an Arby's "restaurant" an unorthodox place to plan your uprising, but their curly fries are also kind of, mostly tasty. BONUS: If you wish to torture your enemies, simply take them an Arby's and force them to eat the curly fries.

Haunted carnivals

Self-explanatory.

The top of the Golden Gate Bridge

This may seem like a ludicrous idea, but when was the last time you saw the police hanging out at the top of the Golden Gate Bridge? Aside from Thursdays?

A shark tank

On the one hand, nobody would dare get into a shark tank, so you'll be completely alone to plan your revolution. On the other hand, the shark will probably kill you. On the other *other* hand, (you have three hands), dying while in the midst of a revolution makes you a martyr.

Now you know where you should plan your revolution. But what should the revolutionary meeting location actually include? Due to the modern age in which we live, the revolution room must provide access to the world around you. The idyllic revolution meeting space will be equipped with at least fourteen televisions: two televisions that only play CNN, three televisions that only play Fox News, and nine televisions that only play TBS — so that nobody misses an episode of *Seinfeld*. In addition to the fourteen televisions, the modern revolution meeting location should also include:

- 20 computers that search the Internet for news, porn, and news about porn
- 8 subscriptions to *The New York Times*
- 1 book titled *How to Fold a Newspaper Into a Hat*
- 17 maps — the more 3D, the better

• 34 air fresheners, because the previous renters took in stray cats

And of course, you'll want to stock up on plenty of guns. Unless you're planning a *nonviolent* revolution, in which case you'll need to stock up on flowers (preferably the poisonous kind).

Up to this point, you have now:

1. Defined what your revolution is.
2. Figured out a name for your revolution.
3. Created a slogan for your revolution.
4. Held a meeting in which you rallied together your fellow political activists for your revolution.
5. Applied for all the applicable permits and licenses for your revolution.
6. Not gotten a haircut for your revolution.[154]

154. You hippie.

❓ A REVOLUTIONARY QUIZ ❓

Revolution planning meetings should always begin with:

A) A prayer.

B) A poem.

C) A moment of silence.

D) A human sacrifice to the Hebrew god Ba'al, followed by a roasted tomato basil soup and a light shaved fennel salad.

Can you feel it? There's something in the air. No, I'm not talking about the stench from the tomato-paste processing factory down the street. What you're feeling in the air are the winds of change. Something big is about to happen, and you are about to become a part of it. Are you nervous? You should be. Are you scared? That's only natural. Are you wetting your pants? Now you're just being childish.

THE HOUR OF PREPARATION HAS PASSED.

THE REVOLUTION IS NOW UPON US.

I NEED TO FIX THE CAPS LOCK ON THIS COMPUTER.

Intensity Level 1: Letters & Petitions

Intensity Level 1 Letters & Petitions	Intensity Level 2 Protests & Rallies	Intensity Level 3 Riots & Violence

Every revolution begins with just one complaint. Sometimes this is in the form of a letter to a friend, complaining of the oppressive way in which the city council has cracked down on smoking in city parks and the public stoning of harlots. Other times it is in the form of a signed petition, asking a local company, Pollutions 'R Us, Inc., to cease dumping their pollution in the river. Whatever the cause and whatever the issue, the revolution will always begin with just a single complaint. It's also possible for the original complaint to be accompanied by many other complaints, especially if the person doing the complaining is imbibing alcohol, or is your mother-in-law.[155]

155. And now you know why 97 percent of all revolutions are started by alcoholics. Or your mother-in-law.

Although complaining about a problem or issue can take many forms, the most common form is that of the *letter*. Many people are surprised to learn that something as simple as a letter can carry a lethal dose of potency. What these people don't realize is that seven out of ten mail carriers in the United States die every year from arsenic poisoning.[156]

Coincidence?

You've written your letter of complaint, and it's been signed, sealed, delivered,[157] but where exactly was your letter delivered and in what form? The following are examples of letters from history, demonstrating the number of places where you may voice your concerns:

- **A Letter to the Editor:** This may seem like a simple and antiquated idea, but it took only one letter to the editor printed in the Italian newspaper, *Il Newspaper Italiano*, for Benito Mussolini to come into power and eventually lead the National Fascist Party. His letter was also the inspiration behind the comic strip, *Garfield*.[158]

- **An Open Letter:** This type of letter is what you sometimes see in popular national news magazines, such as *TV Guide* or *High Times*. Spanish revolutionary Simón Bolívar, who went by the nickname Simón José Antonio de la Santísima Trinidad Bolívar y Palacios Ponte Blanco, was known for his many open letters in *The New Yorker*, as well as his reviews of New York theatre.

- **An Anonymous Letter, Haphazardly Copied**

156. Hence the term poisoned pen letter.

157. I'm yours.

158. Ever notice that Garfield always ate lasagna — an *Italian* food?

on a Malfunctioning Copier and Posted on Telephone Poles Around Town: The Irish Rebellion of 1798 (which actually occurred in 1812, and should not to be confused with the War of 1812, which won't take place until 3047) started when Henry Joy McCracken, a founding member of the Society of the United Irishmen, began stapling copies of his strongly-worded letter to King George III on telephone poles, cutting telephone service for everyone in his neighborhood.

• **A Mass E-mail:** The Belgian Revolution began when a disgruntled employee at a paper distributor accidentally clicked on "reply all" instead of "reply;" thus sending out his resignation e-mail to all 3,000 employees in his company. It didn't help that his e-mail included an attachment of a video showing Erasme Louis Surlet de Chokier eating a Belgian waffle off his hotel room floor in the nude.

A REVOLUTIONARY FUN FACT!

The pen is mightier than the sword. Especially if the pen shoots bullets.

There is nothing more American about America than signing a petition.[159] It was a petition that brought us the Declaration of Independence in 1776, it was a petition that ended the Civil War in 1865, it was a petition that dropped the atomic bomb in 1945, and it was a petition that made signing petitions illegal in 1987. Signing a petition is the easiest, most passive way in which a person may become involved in a political cause, an important issue, or a strongly held belief, thus making petition-signing a very, very important part of a revolution.

Let's say, for example, that you want to overthrow the Canadian government.[160] As simple as overthrowing the Canadian government may sound (Skill Level: 7), you certainly won't be able to do it on your own. You've probably been taught since you were young that one person cannot make a difference, and this is true for two reasons: 1. There is strength in numbers, and 2. Don't ever bother voting.

Now imagine that the Canadian government received a petition of 50,000 signatures, stating that they were about to be overthrown. Would they take such a threat seriously? It doesn't matter, because this is the Canadian government we're talking about here. The point is, you would be successful in your endeavor, simply because you have enough people who agree with you. And as an added bonus, you also now have a mailing list which can be sold to marketers and people who send out spam.[161]

You want to collect thousands, upon tens of signatures. But what kind of information do you need to collect with

159. Except for apple pie, according to the signatures of 5,000 people in the tri-county area.

160. One of the very few governments that can be overthrown before the 6:00 evening news.

161. Little known revolutionary fact: Revolutionaries are always interested in penile enhancement pills, fake Rolodex watches, and making fast cash. Always.

your little clipboard there? Are names and signatures good enough? What if you want to contact them by phone? You'll probably need to collect their phone number. What if you want to contact them at their home? Then you'll probably want to collect their home addresses as well. What if you want to know how many children they have under the age of six? Then you're probably a creep, and most likely shouldn't be standing outside of Toys-R-Us with a clipboard.

Just as revolutions are as varied as the sands on the beach or the stars in the wherever-it-is-that-stars-are, so too are the types of petitions. If you plan to overthrow the government through violent means, then you will need to know whether those signing your petition throw a right punch or a left punch. If you're a peace activist who's trying to collect enough signatures to convince two different nations to sign a peace treaty, then you will need to know whether those signing prefer a punch in the face with a right punch or a left punch.[162]

162. Hint: Try both

The following are a few examples of different petitions, each containing the different questions and information you should (or should not, depending on your arthritis) be asking.

	Name	Phone	Address	Email	Political Party
1					
2					
3					

	Name	I agree that marijana should be legalized	I disagree that marijuana should be legalalized	Sorry, I'm kind of stoned right now. What was the question again? Has anyone ever mentioned you look like Don Knotts?
1				
2				
3				

	What's your name?	Are you single?	What's your sign?	Oh, baby.
1				
2				
3				

	Name	Chocolate?	Vanilla?	Sprinkles?!
1				
2				
3				

	Name	Social Security No.	Pin	Mother's Maiden Name
1				
2				
3				

	Name	Ann Landers	Dear Abby	No thank you, I know how to take care of my own problems.
1				
2				
3				

	Name	You say pot-ay-to!	I say po-tah-to!	Over one million people died during the Great Potato Famine in Ireland.
1				
2				
3				

Intensity Level 2: Protests & Rallies

Intensity Level 1 Letters & Petitions	**Intensity Level 2** **Protests & Rallies**	Intensity Level 3 Riots & Violence

There's an old joke that goes: "What's the opposite of progress? *Congress*." I however don't find it very funny. I think the original, unadulterated joke was much funnier: "What's the opposite of development and growth? *An elected representative*."

Comedygold™.

If the opposite of Congress is progress, and the opposite of Tim Conway is Tim Proway, then the opposite of a contest is a *protest*.[163] Protesting is the very heart of any revolution, and to throw a revolution without a protest is like trying to get blood from a turnip that isn't bleeding all that much. Taking to the streets and protesting is the gasoline in your revolution automobile — without it, you probably wouldn't have a revolution. Or you would just ride a bike.[164]

The reason behind protesting is disobedience and non-compliance. Think back to when you were a child, to when your parents told you not to do something, such as eat lots of candy before bedtime, or put the kitten in the microwave. What would you do to get your way? You would throw a tantrum until you got your way, followed by a lie saying that the kitten must have run away, and no, you don't know what that awful burning smell is. Protesting is not unlike throwing a tantrum. The government says, "we rigged the

163. Ironically, most people who lose contests end up protesting

164. Or you would just buy an electric car if you're Ed Begley, Jr.

election and there's nothing you can do about it," and so you respond by taking to the streets, protesting, and chanting "How did that dead kitten get in the microwave? How did that dead kitten get in the microwave?" If you want to revolt, then you'll have to protest. That tantrum isn't going to throw itself.

You will be surprised to learn[165] that there are many different types of protests. Some are stationary, known as "rallies." Others are mobile, known as "marches." Others are even a combination of the two, known as "Segways." One of the more popular forms of protesting that has sprung up over the years is that of the "peace camp," although nearly everyone will agree that this is an ineffective and lazy way to protest.[166] Other forms of protesting include lock-downs, walkouts, blackouts, shout-outs, dropouts, campouts, burnouts, cookouts, die-ins, sit-ins, teach-ins, break-ins, coffins, muffins, *Rowan & Martin's Laugh-In*, and tax resistance. While a combination of any of these methods may be effective for your revolution, only one of these involves Goldie Hawn in a bikini.[167]

Sometimes the goals of a revolution will be satisfied through little more than a really serious e-mail campaign and a couple of handshakes.[168] Sometimes though, the goals of a revolution will only be accomplished after brute force, such as cutting off ears, and shoving really hard.

The methods that can be used in protesting range from the most passive to the most aggressive, as seen here:

165. Unless you've read ahead.

166. Everybody? Everybody.

167. Tax resistance.

168. *Firm handshakes.*

Peace Camp · Tax Resistance · Boycott · Die-in · Sit-in · Teach-in · Public Nudity · Your Mother-in-Law · Hunger Strike · Walkout · Strike & Picketing · Occupation · Rally · Marches

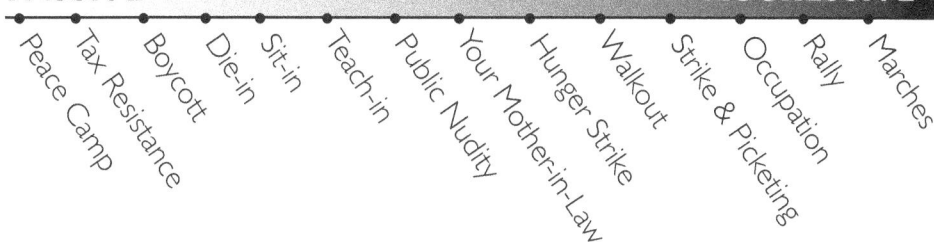

It is important to note that not all methods will be applicable in all revolutions. Also, while the scope of the following protest methods is enough to fill a book, these should be considered only summaries. Poor summaries, at that.

Peace Camp

If you spend your days sitting around in tents, eating vegan hummus, smelling flowers, and playing your ukulele — all in the name of promoting peace — odds are that you live in a peace camp. Peace camps rarely accomplish anything worthwhile in a revolution. This is because most of the revolutionaries living in peace camps are too busy braiding each other's hair and pretending to be Adam and Eve to actually get anything done. In fact, peace camps are not all that dissimilar to the actual Garden of Eden, with the exception that the Garden of Eden had an *actual* talking snake, and peace camps only have peyote.

Tax Resistance

Resisting to pay one's taxes is a method of protesting employed by many revolutionaries, including the radical reformer, Wesley Snipes. Most people participating in tax resistance do so out of opposition to a government's policies. However, the method is rather passive, because many people end up tax resisting without even realizing they're doing so. In fact, I'm protesting right now and don't even realize it.

Boycott

Revolutionaries who disagree with the business practices of a corporation sometimes participate in a boycott, where everyone agrees to refrain from buying from a particular company. Boycotts aren't always successful, as protestors tend to wane in their participation over time. For example, liberal arts college students have been boycotting jobs since the 1830s.

Die-In

Those revolutionaries protesting a war or cigarettes will often take part in die-ins, where several people lay down and pretend to be dead, symbolically representing the lives of those taken prematurely. Others who are known for pretending to be dead are those who drink too much on New Year's Eve and pass out.

Sit-In

A sit-in is very similar to a die-in, but instead of pretending to be dead, you pretend to be sitting up. Sit-ins are sometimes known as "sit-down strikes," due to the fact that you just arrived to the strike after a long day at work, and are too tired to stand around. This type of protesting was a favorite of Franklin D. Roosevelt's and Dr. Strangelove's.

Teach-In

Remember that substitute teacher you hated when you were young? She always punished you by making you miss recess, or by forcing you to watch anti-Vietnam War propaganda films, followed by a panel that refused to limit the discussion to a specific frame of time or academic scope of topic? Your substitute teacher was engaging in a "teach-in," a method used by revolutions to instruct protestors on the issues relating to the revolution. Such methods were popular during the 1960s, as well as anytime a substitute teacher arrived to school *with* a hangover and *without* a teacher's manual.

Public Nudity

Some revolutionaries believe public nudity is a useful tool when protesting, and these revolutionaries are absolutely correct. Public nudity is sometimes used to protest a government's indecency laws, sometimes public nudity is used by PETA to symbolically demonstrate cruelty to animals, and all times public nudity is fantastic. PLEASE NOTE: You should not participate in public nudity if you are not attractive.[169]

169. Sorry, but I don't make the rules.

Your Mother-In-Law

There isn't a more perfect balance of passive-aggressiveness than your mother-in-law. She compliments you on your wardrobe, and then tells you how to raise your children. She'll offer to lend you money, but then complain that you're always milking her for financial help. Employ your mother-in-law in your revolution, and your side will come out victorious.[170]

170. Every single time.

Hunger Strike

Going on a hunger strike is a method of nonviolent resistance, in which the protestor abstains from food with the sole purpose of provoking guilt in others. It's also a great way to lose weight, because hunger strikes are only effective if they're made public — nobody's going to go off a diet with all those cameras pointed at them.[171] The concept of a hunger strike first became well publicized by Mahatma Gandhi, who learned of the method from a supermodel he was dating at the time.

171. Just ask Oprah.

Walkout

A walkout is when many people leave a place of employment or an organization en masse, to demonstrate their disapproval over the aforementioned company or organization's policies or behavior. While it may be fun to have a day off work, the downside of a walkout is that you'll most likely be fired and/or get shin splints.

Strike & Picketing

172. As an added bonus of cleaning out the garage, you'll finally have a place to park the car.

You have a garage full of picket signs collecting dust — why not clean out the garage and put those picket signs to good use?[172] Striking involves walking back and forth in front of a corporation, a government building, or other institution in a wide variety of patterns: circles, figure eights, squares, obtuse triangles, and tetrahedrons. The reason for striking is to let your opposition know that you're opposed to their policies, that you are capable of yelling without getting a hoarse voice (Sorry, Carol Channing, no picketing for you), and that you're a very good sign maker. Government entities and other organizations are always impressed by sign making, which is why Kinko's wins every revolution in which they're involved.

Occupation & Lock-Down

Occupying, or locking-down, is a method of protesting in which you refuse to move from a certain location or object. Environmentalists are known to utilize lock-downs, since the method gives them an excuse to chain themselves to a tree without looking absolutely and legitimately insane. Chaining yourself to a tree, while claiming to defend your favorite environmental political cause, is also a popular way to come in contact with termites. Locking-down is usually employed in green revolutions and sexual revolutions, although not for the reasons you might think.[173]

Rally

A rally is a gathering of people who assemble because of a common political goal or issue. Usually this assembly takes place in a strategic or symbolic place, such as the steps of the state capitol, or a laundromat.[174] The number

173. If an environmentalist chains himself to a tree and nobody hears his sounds, does he have a protest?

174. Both are great locations to get a load of clothes washed.

of people at a rally can be as many as a million, or as few as only two, although technically a gathering of only two people is considered a "date."

The rally is where you will put into practice the techniques you have learned throughout this book, such as:

- Song singing.
- Sign waving.
- Fist shaking.
- At people yelling.

Unfortunately, all rallies must also have at least a few boring speeches. A necessary evil, boring speeches serve a dual purpose: they inspire other people at the rally, and help the speaker achieve a level of self-importance that is required for all revolutionaries. For example, Bhagat Singh, a freedom fighter in the Indian independence movement who died in 1931, became a revolutionary only after giving a PowerPoint presentation, which demonstrated the pros and cons of the Indian independence movement. Even Martin Luther King Jr. didn't become a successful civil rights activist until he gave his famous "I Had the Craziest Dream Last Night"[175] speech.

175. After a night of heavy drinking.

HOW TO GIVE A MEMORABLE SPEECH

Follow these steps to give a memorable and revolutionary speech, if you wish to be remembered for all of history:

1. Begin with a joke or an anecdote. Some of the tried-and-tested introductions include:

- Four-score-and-seven years ago …
- Thanks, you look like a great audience …
- I just flew here and boy, are my arms tired …
- A rabbi, a priest, and a minister walk into a bar …

2. **Transition into the actual theme of your speech, which should relate to the purpose of your revolution. Use some of the following examples, or come up with your own:**
   - But seriously folks …
   - That reminds me, what's the deal with capitalism …
   - Men and women proletariats sure are different, aren't they …
   - So the rabbi says to the priest …

3. **Provide a clear and concise target against which your fellow revolutionaries will direct their anger. You may use any of these as a transition:**
   - You know what really chaps my hide …
   - Is it just me, or have you ever noticed that the proletariat is being run down by the aristocratic government …
   - We have nothing to fear but fear itself. And snakes …
   - In other words, it's the minister's fault …

4. **After presenting the target or problem in your speech, provide your fellow revolutionaries with a realistic goal, such as the following:**
   - And after we bring down our boss, our department,

and our company, our next mission will be to get rid of Mondays …

- You bring the pitchforks, and you bring the torches, and you bring the water bottles and orange wedges …
- So who's with me? Anyone else want to defend the Alamo against the Mexican Army? C'mon, what could possibly go wrong? Afterwards, I'll give everyone their choice of tickets for a free ride on the Hindenburg or the Titanic …
- But after the priest had a few drinks, he started to get a little drunk …

5. **Conclude your speech with a stirring, memorable line:**
   - And that, ladies and gents, is why I hate turquoise jewelry.
   - Thank you, you've been a lovely audience! Don't forget to tip your waitress.
   - Who else wants to depose the government of its tyrannical leader? No? OK, then, who wants to go catch a movie?
   - And the rabbi says, "That's not a duck, that's my mother-in-law!"

Marches

According to a recent survey in *Cat Fancy*, 87 percent of all revolutionary rallies eventually evolve into marches, which is why an understanding of marching patterns will come in handy. You don't necessarily have to use marching patterns when moving your masses against your targeted opponent, but those who march without a plan or formation usually end up lost somewhere downtown, actually joining the enemy, or worst, going home to take a nap.

The following marching block formations will give you some good ideas on how to organize, and have been approved and certified by both J.P. Souza and the Macy's Thanksgiving Day Parade committee:

Two Single Columns Block Formation
Two groups of blocks will line up parallel to march down the street. Good for squeezing through narrow spaces.

Four Double Lapping Half Block Formation
Eight groups will form, with four on top and four on the bottom. This formation is used when the purpose of the march is to fill an entire street.[176]

Two Single Columns Plus Two Half Circles Formation
Two groups will form two long columns, while four groups form two small blocks and half circles, as seen here. This marching pattern is best used when protesting outside of a bank.

176. If this formation is used during a Gay Pride protest march, the tops will be on the top row, and the bottoms will be on the … well, you get the idea.

Four Columns Plus One Long Column In the Middle Block Formation:

Four shorter columns are formed, with a longer column in the middle. This formation is used often in revolutions, and is more successful if accompanied by birds, but flipped upside down.

Thirty-Seven Blocks to Form the Shape of Three Women Who Fight Crime Formation

Individual groups of revolutionaries form, to create a formation that resembles women who fight crime for a boss they've never met. It should be pointed out that this formation usually sets the women's rights movement back by a decade or so.

Eighteen Blocks to Form the Shape of a Guy Listening to an MP3 Player Formation

This formation is formed by eighteen marchers, who come together to create the shape of some dude rocking out to an MP3 player. It is also one of the more overpriced marching patterns.

Some Horror Director

Nine groups form to display the silhouette of a famous horror director, believed to be either John Carpenter, Wes Craven, or Joel Schumacher.

A WARNING ABOUT "CIVIL DISOBEDIENCE"

Doesn't the idea of civil disobedience sound exciting, in addition to sounding like an oxymoron? Of course it does, you're a revolutionary. As everyone knows, a revolutionary cannot refrain from civil disobeying, anymore than a zebra can change its stripes (unless it undergoes a skin graft). Nevertheless, civil disobedience no longer carries the same punch it used to in the 1960s or the 1790s. The civil disobedience of yesterday is a lot different than the civil disobedience of today. Assuming you live in the present.[177]

The concept of civil disobeying has been greatly watered down recently, due to it being quite widespread throughout our society. In fact, it appears that many people no longer recognize the difference between civil disobeying and aggressively complying. Everybody it seems is civil disobeying these days. Civil disobeying is not unlike the word "cool" – what was once used by a select *few*, is now used by a select *tons of people*.

In fact, civil disobeying is so easy to do nowadays, that it's quite possible you're civil disobeying this very moment and don't even realize it. If any of the following apply to you, you are civil disobeying:
- If you flush the toilet too many times
- If you are under 4'7" or over 6'3"
- If you are allergic to pine nuts
- If you think Benedict Arnold had the right idea
- If you always get twins confused
- If you think *Stop! Or My Mom Will Shoot*[178] was underrated

See what I mean? Odds are, at least twelve out of seven items in the above list are applicable to your own life, meaning that you're civil disobeying *while reading this book*.[179] So, while civil disobedience may be a useful tool in a revolution, you are wise to understand that it is in fact a very rusty, old, and useless tool.[180]

---

177. And you may not. A surprisingly high number of revolutionaries are time travelers.
178. This movie was underrated.
179. Which, may I point out, is a good way to get a paper cut.
180. Kind of like your ex-husband.

Intensity Level 3: Riots & Violence

Intensity Level 1 Letters & Petitions	Intensity Level 2 Protests & Rallies	Intensity Level 3 Riots & Violence

You've done everything possible. You've asked your enemies nicely. You've given them baked goods. You've offered to babysit their children. You've recommended a good car mechanic. You've given them a coupon you found in the PennySaver. You've even taken them to the dentist, no matter how much they complained "I don't have a toothache," and "By the way, why am I bound and gagged?"

You've tried diplomacy with your enemies. You've written them angry letters. You've attended political rallies. You've protested in the streets. You burned an effigy of them. You've tried killing them with kindness.[181] You've tried using the democratic process, without any success (and now you have a bunch of useless campaign buttons).

The government won't listen to you? The corporations won't listen to you? The weird church down the street where they dance with snakes won't listen to you? Helen Keller won't listen to you?[182] You've tried everything you can think of, to no avail. Your peaceful revolution isn't going as well as you had anticipated, and the majority of your revolutionaries are bored.

It's time for a *violent* revolution.

This is the point in the book where the actual magic

181. Nothing says, "Killing them with kindness," like offering them a poisoned cupcake.

182. It might help if she took those iPod headphones out of her ears.

happens. Now to clarify, when I say, "Where the magic happens," I'm not referring to the making of babies. This is the point where you learn whether a right jab to the face is more effective than a left knee thrust to the groin.[183] This is where you will learn whether you should use your own decapitating knife when decapitating a government official — or whether you should purchase one from Costco.[184] You have many choices when it comes to how you will demonstrate your oppressive and fearsome nature, but only one thing is certain: BLOODSHED IS THE KEY. Unless you're a germaphobe.[185] In which case, only one thing is certain: BLOODSHED IS THE KEY, FOLLOWED BY A HARD SCRUBBING AND A STRONG ANTI-DISINFECTANT.

183. Hint: Nothing is more effective than a knee thrust to the groin.

184. Hint: Decapitating knives are sold at Costco in bulk, and usually come with a coupon for peanut butter.

185. Have you ever noticed that germaphobes never offer a helping hand?

A REVOLUTIONARY FUN FACT!

Just because John Lennon and Yoko Ono held two week-long "Bed-Ins for Peace" in 1969 to protest the Vietnam War and promote peace, doesn't mean that they had to stop showering. I mean, seriously.

Before we discuss various methods of rioting and violence, it is important first to understand what you should actually bring to your revolution:

Cyanide Pill

Anti-Cyanide Pill

Oversized Musket

Placard Sign

POWER TO THE PEOPLE! BUT ONLY TO THE PEOPLE THAT AGREE WITH ME!

Spare Change

Banana In Your Pocket

Radioactive Warning

Hammer Pants

RADIOACTIVE 7

Pile of Skulls

Bottle of Gatorade

WHAT YOU SHOULD BRING TO YOUR REVOLUTION

An Oversized Musket

Engaging in a revolution requires the use of a weapon. Not only has the oversized musket been used by revolution- aries more than any other weapon, but the larger the size, the more it will overcompensate for your less-than-average manhood. Remember: size = success.

Cyanide Pill (Right Molar)

Unfortunately, not all revolutionaries are successful. Sometimes revolutionaries find themselves captured by the enemy, or worse, bored. To avoid being tortured, inevitable death, or yet another Sunday at your in-laws, simply bite into the cyanide pill you've discreetly planted in your right molar, sit back, and relax.[186]

186. Just ignore the violent convulsions. They'll pass.

Anti-Cyanide Pill (Left Molar)

Let's admit it, we all make stupid mistakes. Whether it's forgetting to mail the cable bill on time or biting down on the cyanide pill planted in our molar resulting in a quick death, we all have errors we would like to take back. Concealing an anti-cyanide pill in your left molar will prevent the poison from the cyanide pill from having any affect. As an added bonus, cyanide and anti-cyanide pills, when taken together, have a surprising peanut butter and chocolate after taste.

Placard Sign

The placard sign: the quintessential tool of the revolutionary. When swung at a 45° angle, it also becomes the quintessential weapon of the revolutionary.

Banana In Your Pocket

When your enemies ask, "Is that a banana in your pocket or are you just glad to see me," respond with "No, it's just a regular banana. Want a bite?" When they say "Yes," hand them the banana into which you've lodged several cyanide pills. After they die, say, "Now that you're dead, I am in fact glad to see you." Then laugh heartily.

Hammer Pants

Very useful in case you find yourself falling from a plane, or in a plot which involves an MC Hammer impersonation contest, an assassination of a high-ranking politician, and a banana (lodged with cyanide pills).[187]

187. Only to be used during hammer time.

Bottle of Gatorade

In case you get thirsty. Try to stay away from the "blue" flavors, as blue generally isn't found in nature, and tastes like pee.

Pile of Skulls

Nothing is more intimidating than a person standing on a pile of skulls;[188] this will strike fear into the deep recesses of your enemies' hearts. You can acquire skulls from the heads of former enemies, or purchase them at your local party store.

188. Plus balancing on skulls is a good workout for the glutes and abs.

Radioactive Warning

I don't know about you, but I generally stay away from anyone wearing a radioactive sign.

Spare Change

In case you drop your cell phone in a toilet and have to make a call from a payphone. Don't laugh, it happens. Spare change is also useful in case you have to take the bus.

ITEMS TO BRING TO YOUR REVOLUTION, NOT SEEN HERE

Obviously not all items are physical or visible (for

example: invisible items). The following are things that, although not physical, should be brought to your revolution:

Wi-Fi

Most revolutions come equipped with laptops, but you will have to bring your own wi-fi. Having a connection to the internet is necessary; otherwise you will have no way of staying in communication with other revolutionaries, or checking upcoming movie times.

A Broad Knowledge of Pig Latin

Nothing says, "I'm here to depose the head of your nation" more effectively than, "I'may erehay otay eposeday ethay eadhay ofay ouryay ationnay." This is because while your opponents translate what exactly it is you're saying, you're busy deposing the head of the nation.

Tolerance for Chinese Buffets

Most revolutionaries — at least until they receive their unemployment checks — are not wealthy. Therefore, you will be eating at a lot of all-you-can-eat buffets. If you don't have a tolerance for Chinese buffets, you will most likely starve. Or go to a different kind of buffet.[189]

189. Golden Corral?

Ice Breaker Games

Nothing is more awkward than getting to know the new people in your revolution. Being prepared with icebreakers will help everyone get to know each other — and maybe even have fun along the way!

Using Violence to Succeed
In Your Revolution

WARNING: NOT APPROPRIATE FOR CHILDREN

Do not read the following section if you are a child, have a heart condition, happen to be pregnant, use a wheelchair, own a Chia Pet, or cried during the movie "The Prince of Tides."

This is the point of no return. There are no connecting flights, all the taxi drivers have gone home for the night, and the train that would have taken you home has derailed. There is no direction for you to head but forward. Unless you're walking backwards.[190] If you have a squeamish stomach, I suggest you skip this section, close the book, take a few Tums, and lay down. By the way, part of the reason you feel squeamish is because of that bad Chinese food you had last night.

You may be inclined to think that resorting to violence in order to achieve a political goal is desperate. You are correct. Desperate times call for measures that also happen to simultaneously be desperate. The following are violent

190. Why didn't I think of that?

methods that will help you in succeed in, and ultimately end your revolution. For further information, read Sun Tzu's *The Art of War*, preferably one of the pop-up editions. Watching anime cartoons is also helpful, because many of the cartoons are not only graphic, but have female characters with inappropriate cleavage.[191]

The following violent methods are rated in black eyes,[192] with the number of black eyes corresponding to the level of violence. I must point out that I do not condone any of the following methods, and simply list them here as suggestions. That having been said, I can however assure you that not only will these methods work, but they will really, really work.

Lastly, be sure only to engage in the following violent methods if you have the proper protection (a helmet, a hockey mask, a condom, etc.).

Intimidation

People are intimidated by a number of different things. Some people are intimidated by wealth, education, and intelligence,[193] while others are intimidated by threats, warning, and perceived violence. The key to intimidation is to let the person you're intimidating know that you mean business, such as wearing a lucha libre mask and playing a tambourine. It's best if you smell like sulfur.

Destroying Private Property

Destroying private property is a form of intimidation, especially if you leave a note that says, "Now imagine if

191. Believe me, having cleavage in a revolution is more useful than you might think.

192. The author claims no ownership of the following black eyes, and has refused to press charges. The whole thing was a simple misunderstanding.

193. For example, I was once really intimidated by a co-worker, because he was as smart as a whip. Well, at least as smart as a whip who's been to college.

this mailbox had been your head!" (Note: does not work if you leave the note *inside* the mailbox). Be sure to target the private property of important individuals — such as the president, CEO, religious leader, etc. — since destroying the private property of random individuals is not only ineffective, but is a waste of a perfectly good baseball bat.

Destroying a System or Utility

All governments, societies, corporations, religious bodies, and other organizations depend on a delicate combination of factors in order to survive. Any disruption in electricity, water, sewage, mail, agriculture, internet, and other similar utilities can have serious consequences. Time to break out the Molotov cocktails!

Don't be afraid to be creative when deciding on taking out the framework of your opposition. Does your opposition depend on a steady stream of baked potatoes to survive? Then destroy the potato farms. Can they not survive without bottled water? Then destroy the bottling plants. If they depend on overpriced porcelain and batik pillows, then destroy Pier 1. If they depend on hollandaise sauce, then destroy butter, lemon juice, egg yolks, salt, and cayenne pepper.[194] If they depend on happiness and joy, destroy adorable puppies. If they depend on Ragtime music, destroy Scott Joplin. If they depend on breathing, destroy oxygen. If they depend on futuristic dreams that will never happen in our lifetimes, destroy jet propulsion packs. I think you see where I'm going with this.

194. And don't serve warm over asparagus, unless you want it to be delicious.

Destroying a Symbolic Building, Statue, or Symbol

Destroying a church, statue, mosque, temple, or other related building or symbol can have a powerful affect on the opposition in a revolution, since politics and religion are often intertwined with one another. Yes, it's true — politics and religion make for very peculiar bedfellows.[195] Why is this? This is primarily due to the fact that politics always tries to steal the covers, while religion usually wakes up at least three or four times a night to pee.

195. What symbols do in the privacy of their bedrooms should not be legislated.

Public Riot

You never thought you were the type to participate in a riot, did you?[196] You're not one to join unruly violent mobs. The one thing you've always prided yourself on is the fact that you are always in control. As you will soon learn though, *nobody* can avoid a mob, just as nobody can eat only one Lay's potato chip.[197] A riot represents a tipping point in any revolution, as it's impossible to avoid jumping on the bandwagon when everyone else is doing it. Before you jump on the bandwagon, there are a number of questions you must ask yourself: "How much does a bandwagon cost?" and "Where can I find a bandwagon?" Home Depot is a good place to start.

196. This is assuming you're not a Lakers fan.

197. Little known revolutionary fact: Lay's are made out of cocaine.

Kidnapping

Being kidnapped is kind of a bummer. Kidnapping someone else, however, is pretty great. Whisking away the offspring of the leader of your opposition — or even the leader himself — can make you a lot of money if your revolution is broke, and can also be a powerful way of saying, "The individual who kidnapped your child is on the phone. Will you accept the collect call?"

Torture

As has been mentioned earlier in this book, torture is a rare paradox: it is frowned upon in polite company, but is inflicted with complete abandon upon the servants. Torture, like shopping for a new calendar[198] or celebrating Independence Day,[199] has both a time and a place. For example, during the middle of a revolution, torture is appropriate. During a wedding, it is not appropriate.[200]

There are a number of reasons why torture may be inflicted on another person, including:

- Acquiring pertinent information
- Making a political and symbolic gesture
- Your therapist is on vacation
- SERIOUSLY, WHO DOESN'T WASH OUT A TUPPERWARE CONTAINER BEFORE RETURNING IT?! WHAT ARE YOU, A BARBARIAN?! I'M GOING TO PULL YOUR FINGERNAILS OFF, ONE BY ONE!!

Before inflicting torture upon an individual, it is important to gather as much medical information about them as possible. Are they diabetic? Do they have a heart condition? Do they have any allergies you should be aware of? After all, you wouldn't want anyone to get *hurt* by the torture.

198. Best during December.

199. Best during December.

200. Unless of course, you're attending the wedding of your ex-wife.

Terrorism

Terrorism has received a rather bad rap over the years, which is quite a shame. Acts of terrorism used to play a significant role in revolutions, until the terrorists of September 11, 2001 ruined it for everyone. Now anytime the IRA wants to innocently blow up a post office or anytime a fundamentalist Christian wants to nonchalantly shoot everybody in an abortion clinic, everyone jumps to the immediate conclusion that these people are terrorists.

It really speaks volumes about the decline of society, when an individual can't commit mass murder in the name of a political cause, without being labeled as a "terrorist." What's next: bank robbery being treated as a *crime*?

Insurgency

An insurgency is "an armed rebellion against a constituted authority," according to a guy I just asked who was wearing a mask and holding a rifle at the state capital. If your revolution gets to the point where it requires a brute militant tactical force, you generally have only two choices: organizing an insurgency or calling The A-Team. Considering that The A-Team is fictional and does not actually exist, you generally have only one choice: organizing an insurgency. Or calling The A-Team.

To organize an insurgency, you will need as much of the following as possible:

- **PEOPLE.** Trying to organize an insurgency with just one person is, as the French say, "really stupid."[201]

201. Except they're making love as they say it.

- **WEAPONS.** Insurgencies have a history of being incredibly violent, and the only way you will be able to continue this stereotype is through weapons.
- **PASSIONATE AND UNCONTROLLABLE ANGER:** This is very helpful in an insurgency. If unavailable, Subdued Introspection will make a comparable substitute.
- **WEAPONS:** Yeah, you're probably going to need a few more weapons.
- **A SECRET PLAN:** The primary difference between a riot and an insurgency is organization (and calories). It is important to know beforehand where you will strike, when the strike will take place, and whether the insurgency will accept American Express.[202]
- **WEAPONS:** Maybe a few more, just in case.

Should you paint your face? If we learned anything from Sir William Wallace, it's that painting your face can be helpful, as long as it's not overdone, and done in a palette that matches your outfit. Should you scream and shout and yell? Only if done in harmony, and not so loud as to wake up the neighbors. Should you hesitate to shoot your opposition through the eye? Probably not.

Assassination

Are you up to the challenge? Are you one of those people who would just kill for a Nobel Peace Prize? Then perhaps your revolution requires an assassination. Sometimes your rebellion will be targeted at a large group of people,

202. Don't leave home without it. Unless you're going swimming. You probably wouldn't want to swim while holding an American Express card.

such as "Canadians," or "People Who Drive Slow on the Freeway." Other times though, your rebellion will be targeted at just one person. Such is the case when rebelling against a dictator, the head of a corporation, a religious leader, or one of the Keebler Elves.[203] When assassinating an individual, it is important to make sure that you *not* ask permission, *not* set-up a specific schedule, and *not* request that the targeted individual respond to your RSVP. History has proven that most people will not RSVP to their own assassination, surprisingly.

Taking out just one important individual can have a devastating effect on your opposition, since losing a leader can send repercussions throughout whatever it is that feel repercussions.[204] Usually assassinating a leader means the immediate downfall of whatever cause, issue, or revolution he or she was leading, with the small exception of Martin Luther King Jr. And Abraham Lincoln. And Harvey Milk. And Benazir Bhutto. And Mahatma Gandhi. And Malcolm X. And Jesus Christ. And thousands of others. To be honest though, these assassinated figures are special circumstances, or outliers, if you will. And everybody knows what outliers are: inliers that have finally come out of the closet.

203. Specifically, E.L. Fudge.

204. Probably a snare drum.

A REVOLUTIONARY FUN FACT!

Approximately 76% of all revolutions end in divorce.

YOUR REVOLUTION WAS SUCCESSFUL. NOW WHAT?

Do you smell what I smell? The aromatic combination of burning garbage, a soiled diaper full of pea soup, a rotting dead dog, and somebody getting a perm? That wonderful smell is none other than the sweet, sweet smell of success. You've successfully overthrown the government, or strong-armed your former employer to pay fairer wages, or convinced an animated group of asexual fantasy characters to waste their time in *World of Warcraft*,[205] or benefited society in some other way. You have successfully lead a revolution, and YOU HAVE MADE HISTORY.

So now what?

Your natural inclination may be to get all cocky about it. I will advise you to avoid this if at all possible. You may find yourself wanting to brag about your revolution while at the bar with your drinking friends. Or, you may find yourself wanting to list, "Successfully organized a revolution," as a skill on your resume. Or worse, you may even find yourself wanting to tell potential dates that you enjoy long walks on the beach, candlelight dinners, and once lead a bloody coup d'état, which is how you got that scar on your abdomen.[206]

The reason you should avoid bragging about such an historical event in your life, is because then people will *expect you to follow up with yet another, greater, society-changing, revolution.* This isn't going to happen. Leading a revolution is very similar to making love to a supermodel in Prague under the alias "Dirk Velázquez" while on a secret mission to steal

205. With the exception of Leeroy Jenkins.

206. Actually, the scar is from your hernia operation. But I won't tell.

nuclear weapon plans from the office of an albino with halitosis — it only happens once per lifetime. Twice, if you're lucky. Telling the world about your great feat will lead the world to believe that you can accomplish an even greater feat and, unfortunately, most people are simply not blessed to have that many feats.[207]

Another reason you must keep the success of your revolution to yourself is because, as I mentioned in Chapter 1, "Revolutionaries do not want people to keep records about them ... this makes it easier for the revolutionary to get away with all sorts of crap." Having fame and fortune may come with its challenges,[208] but none more so than living under the watchful eye of the press and paparazzi. Once you become a famous revolutionary, everyone will want to know who you're dating, or what the next project you're working on is, or what are you in rehab for this time, or why you haven't adopted a baby from Africa like everyone else. And you don't need that kind of pressure.

Thus after your revolution has ended, you will want to keep a low profile. Settle down. Get married. Give birth to those children you've always been bragging out but never actually existed.[209] Build up your 401K. Retire in Florida in a senior community. It's true that a sedate domestic life may not compare to an exciting revolutionary life, but unfortunately all good things must come to an end (with the exception of mono[210]).

You worked hard on your revolution, donating hours upon minutes to a cause you believed in. You led men and

207. With the exception of centipedes.

208. No, not really.

209. One sure sign of determining if you're pregnant? You're at a baby shower, and for some reason you keep receiving gifts with your name on them.

210. Seriously, it stays with you forever.

women in a revolt that bettered your community, your state, and your world. You changed the course of history, and thus deserve now to live a quiet life, basking in the rewards that inevitably follow. You've deserved it.

Unless of course, you were killed during the revolution. Sorry, this book does not have a money-back guarantee.

SECTION III IN REVIEW

★ Acrophobia is the fear of using a dictionary from great heights. I learned this by reading the book *Everything You Wanted to Know About Phobias But Were Afraid to Ask*.

★ There are seventeen ways to skin a cat. Which reminds me: Should I be worried that I haven't seen Mr. Whiskers in a few days?

★ Even revolutionaries have meetings, even cowgirls get the blues, and even Adolf Hitler had a hot, blond girlfriend. So what's *your* excuse?

★ Revolutionary planning locations must always include cappuccino machines, except in times of famine. In which case an automatic drip coffee maker with built in steamer and warming plate will suffice.

★ Some revolutions are started by a letter to the editor, but even more are started by a Dear John letter.

★ The Canadian government was once overthrown by little more than a petition and a homeless guy named Clive.

★ The opposite of Tim Conway is Tim Proway, because it sounds a lot more optimistic.

★ Most protest marches include colorful floats, marching bands, and a Snoopy balloon.

★ Even non-violent revolutions occasionally require violence, otherwise they wouldn't have the word "violent" in their name.

★ You can find a good discount for a cheap assassin if you shop around.

EPILOGUE

★ ★ ★

This Is Not the Beginning of the Book

CONGRATULATIONS. You have just finished reading the most important book you will ever read in your entire life, with the possible exception of *Everybody Poops*. You should be proud of yourself, for reading this book is quite an accomplishment,[211] as not many people have made it as far as you have. That is because those other people are quitters. Or illiterate. Or have a short attention span.[212]

By having finished reading this book, you have started down a path taken by many revolutionaries before you, a path littered with many revolutionaries' discarded hopes, crushed wishes, and broken beer bottles. Like the many revolutionaries who came before you, you will travel the lows and highs of this path, using the knowledge you acquired from this book as your guide. Just be sure to not travel the path at night, because it goes through a bad part of town.

I'm assuming then, that you are reading this epilogue because you have finished the entire book that preceded it, and did not skip ahead to the end. I'm assuming that you are reading this epilogue, because you have filled your revolutionary brain with useful information and useful-er trivia, and *not* because you turned to the end to see if this book is worth purchasing. If you have not read the actual book that precedes this epilogue, STOP RIGHT NOW. This epilogue is for revolutionaries (and their friends, family members, and co-workers) (oh, and their neighbors,

211. Did somebody say Congressional Medal of Honor?

212. Doesn't it seem like everyone has ADHD these day ... hey look over there, it's a butterfly! And look, the butterfly just landed on the shoulder of a doctor writing a prescription for Ritalin!

obstetricians, and religious leaders) (and also their acupuncturists, personal shoppers, and Gary Busey) ONLY. Do not use this epilogue as a sampling of whether you will enjoy the rest of this book. Sorry, but if you can't stand the heat, don't stand in the kitchen next to the microwave. Because microwaves can give you cancer.

As for those of you who actually read this book in the chronological and/or alphabetical order in which it was intended, you will begin to notice a slight change in your body. Simply reading this book will leave you with better posture, mintier breath, and a slightly higher IQ. For most of you, you will also notice small changes in your blood, your hair, and your stool samples.[213] You will feel braver, your stride will be longer, and your vocabulary will have increased by 0.3 percent. *This is because you are becoming a revolutionary.* If, however, you find that none of this is true, it is highly suggested that you consult a physician. Or read the book a second time.[214]

You now possess a special knowledge of revolutions and the world that is possessed by few, but desired by many. Do not share this revolutionary knowledge! This is because, unlike your social security number,[215] your knowledge of revolutions is secret and private. It is not meant to be shared with others, whether internally or externally. If the whole world possessed information on how to throw a revolution, everyone would revolt against everyone else, and you would be left in the corner of the world, wondering why you opened your big mouth. You, and only you, will possess

213. Although *why* you are checking your stool sample is none of my business.

214. Little known revolutionary fact: There are no refunds.

215. 413-97-2845

this knowledge (with the exception of everyone else who has bought this book[216]); therefore it must be guarded with the same intensity usually reserved for guarding something that requires a lot of guards.

216. Thank you, both of you.

I would like to end this epilogue by telling you why I wrote this book. When I first conceived the idea of writing a book about revolutions, it was little more than a dream. I was armed with the understanding that revolutions are important, history always repeats itself, and that most male ladybugs are transvestites. Some, however, ridiculed my idea. "You will fail, because you're nothing but a dreamer!" they laughed. "Who is this, and how did you get my number?" they complained. To those who accuse me of being little more than a dreamer, I say, "I know you are, but what am I?" I'll tell you what I am. I am a revolutionary. A revolutionary who dreams. *How dare they call me a dreamer!*

As I went about writing this book, I endured many challenges, the likes of which have never before been experienced by men.[217] I had to read *other books*, learn *what a revolution is*, and *do some writing*. I worked on this book to the point of absolute exhaustion, which is why I'm not going to write my next book while using a treadmill.

217. Like pregnancy.

My blood, sweat,[218] and tears went into this book, so that you could learn what it means to be a revolutionary.

218. Just kidding. I don't actually sweat.

There you have it. Through my great sacrifices, (this book cost me a toe[219]) you have received the essential tools for overthrowing your oppressors. Because of my love for you, (I didn't even realize we were dating) you have received

219. I will never again sharpen a pencil while barefoot.

the information needed to start a revolution and change the world.

A famous editor and war correspondent during the American Civil War, Francis Pharcellus Church, best summed up why revolutions occur during history, in his 1897 editorial in *The New York Sun*:

> Yes, Virginia, there is a Santa Claus. He exists as certainly as love and generosity and devotion exist, and you know that they abound and give to your life its highest beauty and joy. Alas! how dreary would the world be if there were no Santa Claus. It would be as dreary as if there were no Virginias. Also, did you know that Santa Claus is the reason why violence exists in the world, why your kitten died last month, and why your parents are getting divorced? Santa Claus is the reason why bad things happen to good people. He is directly responsible for all of humanity's wars, riots, and revolutions. Yes, Virginia, there is a Santa Claus. And he hates you.

Now go start your own revolution.

ACKNOWLEDGEMENTS
★ ★ ★

There are a number of wonderful, talented people without whom this book would not have been possible. Or to put it another way, these are the people to blame for this book:

Lani Dame and Renee Pedroza, for their brilliant graphic design and layout.

Anne Younger, for being my insightful editor and for "getting it."

Mark Mitchell, for his help with the title and the very first draft.

Ginny McOmber and the staff of the Salt Lake City Library, for allowing me to work on this ridiculous book during work hours.

Kristen Hintz and Jeremiah Knight, for the best foreword an author could ask for.

Holly Kapherr, for saying I was a funny writer, even when we both knew that was a lie.

Nathan Severin, for his patience, support, and, most importantly, laptop.

Joe Evans of Nobrow Coffee & Tea, for their support.

Ashley Anderson, Aubrey Carruth, Brandy Fox, Misty Fowler, JD Hamil, Valerie Kraml, Kathy Richards, Kristiana Rockne, Jordan Stuhmueller, Johann Van Dyke, and Dave Rumminger, for their opinions, notes, and insight.

Michael Aaron and the *QSaltLake*, for their support and for publishing the first thing I ever wrote, thus introducing the world to a very unfunny writer.

The staff of *The Regal Seagull*, for their patience during my little "hiatus" and/or nervous breakdown.

My wonderful family — Rick, Denise, Kimberly, Dane, Robbie, and Steven — for their eternal love, and for giving me a twisted sense of humor.

Lastly, a special thanks to *The Onion, The Daily Show, The Colbert Report, Saturday Night Live, This American Life, Mad Magazine*, the *Salt Lake City Weekly* and many others, for all rejecting my applications and submissions. Had they not propelled me into a deep pit of depression and discouragement, I probably wouldn't have moved on to a new writing project — this book.

Thank you, all of you

If your name isn't listed here, it's either because I forgot, or because you're dead to me.

IMAGE CREDITS
★ ★ ★

FRONT AND BACK COVER
Lani Dame
Renee Pedroza

BACK COVER
Author as Che Guevara: Ryan Shattuck

SECTION I, II AND III TITLE PAGES
Fist: Renee Pedroza

COUNTRIES AND THEIR REVOLUTIONS
National flags: Flagpedia.net; public domain images

FAMOUS REVOLUTIONARIES
Historical revolutionaries: Wikipedia.org; public domain images

A DO-IT-YOURSELF REVOLUTIONARY PAMPHLET
Pamphlet: Lani Dame
Kitten graphic: Jenny Szabo
Glamour photo of author: Jenny Szabo

FAMILY TREE OF REVOLUTIONS
Family Tree graphic: Ryan Shattuck

QUIZ: WHAT ROLE DO YOU PLAY IN A REVOLUTION?
Boss mug, brain, muscle, dollar sign, and banana peel graphics: Adrian E. Holmes

POPULAR TARGETS IN RECENT REVOLUTIONS
Pie chart: Lani Dame

MARCHES
Marching formations: Ryan Shattuck

WHAT YOU SHOULD BRING TO YOUR RIOT
Rioter with Items: Ryan Shattuck

USING VIOLENCE TO SUCCEED IN YOUR REVOLUTION
Black eye icons: Ryan Shattuck

ALL OTHER GRAPHICS AND IMAGES
Lani Dame